EYEWITNESS TRAVEL
PHRASE BOOK
ITALIAN

REVISED EDITION

DK LONDON

Senior Editor Christine Stroyan
Senior Art Editors Anna Hall, Amy Child
Art Director Karen Self
Associate Publisher Liz Wheeler
Publishing Director Jonathan Metcalf
Proofreading Margherita Doré, in association with
First Edition Translations Ltd, Cambridge, UK
Senior Pre-Producer Andy Hilliard
Senior Producers Gary Batchelor, Anna Vallarino

DK DELHI

Assistant Editor Sugandha Agarwal
Assistant Art Editor
Anukriti Arora
Art Editors Ravi Indiver,
Mansi Agarwal
Senior Art Editor Chhaya Sajwan
Managing Editor Soma B. Chowdhury
Senior Managing Art Editor
Arunesh Talapatra

Production Manager Pankaj Sharma
Preproduction Managers
Sunil Sharma, Balwant Singh
Senior DTP Designers
Tarun Sharma, Shanker Prasad,
Neeraj Bhatia, Ajay Verma

First American edition 2008
This revised edition published in 2017 by
DK Publishing,
345 Hudson Street, New York, New York 10014

Copyright © 2008, 2017 Dorling Kindersley Limited
DK, a Division of Penguin Random House LLC
18 19 20 10 9 8 7 6 5 4 3
005–300208–Jun/2017

A catalog record for this book is available from the Library of Congress.
ISBN: 978-1-4654-6280-0

Printed and bound in China

A WORLD OF IDEAS:
SEE ALL THERE IS TO KNOW
www.dk.com

CONTENTS

INTRODUCTION

This book provides all the key words and phrases you are likely to need in everyday situations. It is grouped into themes, and key phrases are broken down into short sections to help you build a wide variety of sentences. A lot of the vocabulary is illustrated to make it easy to remember, and "You may hear" boxes feature questions you are likely to hear. At the back of the book there is a menu guide, listing about 500 food terms, and a 2,000-word two-way dictionary. Numbers are listed on the last page of the book for quick reference.

NOUNS

All Italian nouns (words for things, people, and ideas) are masculine or feminine. The gender of singular nouns is usually shown by the word for "the": **il** or **lo** (masculine) and **la** (feminine). They change to **l'** before vowels. The plural forms are **i** or **gli** (masculine) and **le** (feminine).

ADJECTIVES

Most Italian adjectives change endings according to whether they describe a masculine or feminine, singular or plural word. In this book the singular masculine form is shown, followed by the alternative feminine ending:

I'm lost   **Mi sono perso/a**

"YOU"

There are two ways of saying "you" in Italian: **lei** (polite) and **tu** (familiar). In this book we have used **lei** throughout, as that is what you normally use with people you don't know.

VERBS

Verbs change according to whether they are in the singular or plural. In phrases where this happens, the singular form of the verb is followed by the plural form:

Where is/are...?   **Dov'è/Dove sono...?**

PRONUNCIATION GUIDE

Below each Italian word or phrase in this book, you will find a
pronunciation guide in italics. Read it as if it were English and
you should be understood, but remember that it is only a guide
and for the best results you should listen to the native speakers in
the audio app and try to mimic them. Some Italian sounds are
different from those in English, so take note of how the letters
below are pronounced.

a	like "a" in "car"
ai	like "i" in "mile"
ao, au	like "ow" in "cow"
c	before "a," "o," and "u," like "k" in "kite" before "i" and "e," like "ch" in "church"
cc	like "ch" in "church"
ch	like "k" in "keep"
e	like "e" in "pet"
ei	like "ay" in "day"
g	before "a," "o," and "u," like "g" in "get" before "i" and "e," like "j" in "jam"
gh	like "g" in "got"
gli	like "lli" in "million"
gn	like "ni" in "onion"
h	silent
i	like "ee" in "keep"
o	like "o" in "pot"
oi	like "oy" in "boy"
qu	like "qu" in "quick"
r	rolled
s	like "s" in "see" or "z" in "zoo"

sc	before "a," "o," and "u," like "sk" in "skip"
	before "i" or "e," like "sh" in "ship"
u	like "oo" in "boot"
z	like "ts" in "pets," or "ds" in "loads"

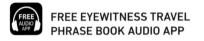

FREE EYEWITNESS TRAVEL PHRASE BOOK AUDIO APP

The audio app that accompanies this phrase book contains nearly 1,000 essential Italian words and phrases, spoken by native speakers, for use when traveling or when preparing for your trip.

HOW TO USE THE AUDIO APP
- Download the free app on your smartphone or tablet from the App Store or Google Play.
- Open the app and scan or key in the barcode on the back of your Eyewitness Phrase Book to add the book to your Library.
- Download the audio files for your language.
- The 🎧 symbol in the book indicates that there is audio for that section. Enter the page number from the book into the search field in the app to bring up the list of words and phrases for that page or section. You can then scroll up and down through the list to find the word or phrase you want.
- Tap a word or phrase to hear it.
- Swipe left or right to view the previous or next page.
- Add phrases you will use often to your Favorites.

ESSENTIALS

In this section, you will find the essential words and useful
phrases you need for basic everyday talk and situations.
Be aware of cultural differences when you're addressing
Italian people, and also remember that they tend to be quite
formal when they are greeting each other, using *signore*
(for men), *signora* (for women), and *signorina* (for girls and
younger women). These titles are also used with last names.

GREETINGS

Hello	Salve *salveh*
Good evening	Buonasera *bwonaserah*
Good night	Buonanotte *bwonanotteh*
Goodbye	Arrivederci *arreevederchee*
Hi/bye!	Ciao/ciao! *chow*
Pleased to meet you	Piacere *pyachereh*
How are you?	Come sta? *komeh stah*
Fine, thanks	Bene, grazie *beneh gratsye*
You're welcome	Prego *pregoh*
My name is...	Mi chiamo... *mee kyamoh*
What's your name?	Come si chiama? *komeh see kyamah*
What's his/her name?	Lui/lei come si chiama? *looee/lay komeh see kyamah*
This is...	Questo/a è... *kwestoh/ah eh*
Nice to meet you	Lieto/a di conoscerla *lyetoh/ah dee konosherlah*
See you tomorrow	A domani *ah domanee*
See you soon	A presto *ah prestoh*

SMALL TALK

Yes/no	Sì/no *see/noh*
Please	Per favore *pehr favoreh*
Thank you (very much)	(Molte) grazie *(molteh) gratsye*
You're welcome	Prego *pregoh*
OK/fine	OK/bene *okay/beneh*
Pardon?	Scusi? *skoozee*
Excuse me	Mi scusi *mee skoozee*
Sorry	Mi dispiace *mee deespyacheh*
I don't know	Non so *non soh*
I don't understand	Non capisco *non kapeeskoh*
Could you repeat that?	Può ripetere? *pwo reepetereh*
I don't speak Italian	Non parlo italiano *non parloh eetalyanoh*
Do you speak English?	Parla inglese? *parlah eenglezeh*
What is the Italian for...?	Come si dice in italiano...? *komeh see deeche een eetalyanoh*
What's that called?	Come si chiama? *komeh see kyamah*
Can you tell me...	Mi può dire... *mee pwoh deereh*

TALKING ABOUT YOURSELF

I'm from...	Vengo da... *vengoh dah*
I'm...	Sono... *sonoh*
...American	...americano/a *amereekanoh/ah*
...English	...inglese *eengleseh*
...Canadian	...canadese *kanadezeh*
...Australian	...australiano/a *owstralyanoh/ah*
...single	...celibe/nubile *cheleebeh/noobeeleh*
...married	...sposato/a *sposatoh/ah*
...divorced	...divorziato/a *deevortsyatoh/ah*
I am...years old	Ho...anni *oh...annee*
I have...	Ho... *oh*
...a boyfriend	...un fidanzato *oon feedantsatoh*
...a girlfriend	...una fidanzata *oonah feedantsatah*
Where are you from?	Da dove viene? *dah doveh vyeneh*
Are you married?	È sposato/a? *eh sposatoh/ah*
Do you have children?	Ha figli? *ah feelye*

SOCIALIZING

Do you live here?	Vive qui? *veeveh kwee*
Where do you live?	Dove vive? *doveh veeveh*
I am here...	Sono qui... *sonoh kwee*
...on vacation	...in vacanza *een vakantsah*
...on business	...per lavoro *pehr lavoroh*
I'm a student	Sono uno/a studente/studentessa *sonoh oonoh/ah stoodente/stoodentessah*
I work in...	Lavoro a... *lavoroh ah*
I am retired	Sono pensionato/a *sonoh pensyonatoh/ah*
Can I have...	Posso avere... *possoh avereh*
...your telephone number?	...il suo numero di telefono? *eel soowoh noomeroh dee telefonoh*
...your email address?	...il suo indirizzo e-mail? *eel soowoh eendeereedzo emayl*
It doesn't matter	Non importa *non eemportah*
Cheers!	Cin cin *cheen cheen*
Do you mind if I smoke?	Le dispiace se fumo? *leh deespyache seh foomoh*
I don't drink/smoke	Non bevo/fumo *non bevoh/foomoh*
Are you alright?	Sta bene? *stah beneh*

LIKES AND DISLIKES

I like/love...	Mi piace/adoro... *mee pyacheh/adoroh*
I don't like...	Non mi piace... *non mee pyacheh*
I hate...	Detesto... *detestoh*
I rather/really like...	Mi piace abbastanza/molto... *mee pyacheh abbastantsa/moltoh*
Don't you like it?	Non le piace? *non leh pyacheh*
I would like...	Vorrei... *vorray*
My favorite is...	Il mio preferito è... *eel meeoh prefereetoh eh*
I prefer...	Preferisco... *prefereeskoh*
I think it's great	Penso che sia fantastico *pensoh keh sya fantasteeko*
It's delicious	È delizioso/a *eh deleetsyozoh/ah*
What would you like to do?	Cosa vorrebbe fare? *kozah vorrebbeh fareh*
I don't mind	Non mi dispiace *non mee deespyacheh*
Do you like...?	Le piace...? *leh pyacheh*

YOU MAY HEAR...

Di cosa si occupa?
dee kozah see okoopah
What do you do?

È in vacanza?
eh een vakantsah
Are you on vacation?

DAYS OF THE WEEK

What day is it today?	Che giorno è oggi? *keh jornoh eh ojee*	**Friday**	venerdì *venerdee*
Sunday	domenica *domeneekah*	**Saturday**	sabato *sabatoh*
Monday	lunedì *loonedee*	**today**	oggi *odjee*
Tuesday	martedì *martedee*	**tomorrow**	domani *domanee*
Wednesday	mercoledì *merkoledee*	**yesterday**	ieri *yeree*
Thursday	giovedì *jovedee*	**in...days**	tra...giorni *trah...jornee*

THE SEASONS

primavera
preemaverah
spring

estate
estateh
summer

MONTHS

January	gennaio *jenayo*	July	luglio *loolyo*
February	febbraio *febrayo*	August	agosto *agostoh*
March	marzo *martso*	September	settembre *setembreh*
April	aprile *apreeleh*	October	ottobre *otobreh*
May	maggio *majjo*	November	novembre *novembreh*
June	giugno *joonyo*	December	dicembre *deechembreh*

autunno
owtoonnoh
fall

inverno
eenvernoh
winter

TELLING THE TIME 🎧

What time is it?	Che ore sono? *keh oreh sonoh*
It's nine o'clock	Sono le nove *sonoh leh noveh*
...in the morning	...del mattino *del matteenoh*
...in the afternoon	...del pomeriggio *del pomereedjoh*
...in the evening	...della sera *dellah serah*

l'una
loonah
one o'clock

l'una e dieci
loonah eh deeaychee
ten past one

l'una e un quarto
loonah eh oon kwartoh
quarter past one

l'una e venti
loonah eh ventee
twenty past one

l'una e mezza
loonah eh medza
half past one

due meno un quarto
dooeh menoh oon kwartoh
quarter to two

due meno dieci
dooeh menoh deeaychee
ten to two

le due
leh dooeh
two o'clock

It's noon/midnight	È mezzogiorno/mezzanotte *eh medzojornoh/medzanotteh*
second	il secondo *eel sekondoh*
minute	il minuto *eel meenootoh*
hour	l'ora *lorah*
a quarter of an hour	un quarto d'ora *oon kwartoh dorah*
half an hour	mezz'ora *medzorah*
three-quarters of an hour	tre quarti d'ora *tray kwartee dorah*
late	tardi *tardee*
early/soon	presto/presto *prestoh*
What time does it start?	A che ora inizia? *ah keh orah eeneetsya*
What time does it finish?	A che ora finisce? *ah keh orah feeneesheh*
How long will it last?	Quanto tempo durerà? *kwantoh tempoh doorerah*

YOU MAY HEAR...

A presto *ah prestoh* **See you later**	È in anticipo *eh een anteecheepoh* **You're early**	È in ritardo *eh een reetardoh* **You're late**

THE WEATHER 🎧

What's the weather like?	Che tempo fa? *ke tempoh fah*
It's...	È... *eh*
...good	...buono *bwonoh*
...bad	...cattivo *kateevoh*
...warm	...mite *meeteh*
...hot	...caldo *kaldoh*
...cold	...freddo *freddoh*

È soleggiato
eh soledjatoh
It's sunny

È piovoso
eh pyovozoh
It's raining

È nuvoloso
eh noovolozoh
It's cloudy

È tempestoso
eh tempestozoh
It's stormy

What's the forecast?	Quali sono le previsioni? *kwalee sonoh leh preveezyonee*
What's the temperature?	Qual è la temperatura? *kwaleh lah temperatoorah*
It's...degrees	Ci sono...gradi *chee sonoh...gradee*
It's a beautiful day	È una bellissima giornata *eh oonah beleesseemah jornatah*
The weather's changing	Il tempo sta cambiando *eel tempoh stah kambyandoh*
Is it going to get colder/ hotter?	Farà più freddo/caldo? *farah pew freddoh/kaldoh*
It's cooling down	La temperatura sta scendendo *lah temperatoorah stah shendendoh*

Nevica
neveeka
It's snowing

È ghiacciato
eh gyatchyatoh
It's icy

C'è nebbia
che nebbyah
It's misty

È ventoso
eh ventozoh
It's windy

GETTING AROUND

Italy has an excellent road system if you are traveling around the country by car, although you have to pay a toll (*un pedaggio*) to use the fast *autostrade* (highways). Italian trains, linking the main towns and cities, are fast, punctual, and surprisingly inexpensive. In large cities you can get around by taxi, bus or tram. In Milan and Rome there is also the subway (*metropolitana*).

ASKING WHERE THINGS ARE

| Excuse me | Mi scusi |
| | *mee skoozee* |

| Where is... | Dov'è... |
| | *doveh* |

| ...the town center? | ...il centro della città? |
| | *eel chentroh dellah cheetah* |

| ...the train station? | ...la stazione ferroviaria? |
| | *lah statsyoneh ferovyarya* |

| ...a cash machine? | ...uno sportello bancomat? |
| | *oonoh sportelloh bankomat* |

| How do I get to...? | Come posso arrivare a...? |
| | *komeh possoh arreevareh ah* |

| I'm going to... | Sto andando a... |
| | *stoh andandoh ah* |

| I'm looking for... | Sto cercando... |
| | *stoh cherkandoh* |

| I'm lost | Mi sono perso/a |
| | *mee sonoh persoh/ah* |

| Is it near? | Si trova qui vicino? |
| | *see trovah kwee veecheenoh* |

| Is there a...nearby? | C'è un...qui vicino? |
| | *che oon...kwee veecheenoh* |

| Is it far? | È lontano? |
| | *eh lontanoh* |

| How far is... | Quanto dista... |
| | *kwantoh deestah* |

| ...the town hall? | ...il municipio? |
| | *eel mooneecheepyo* |

| ...the market? | ...il mercato? |
| | *eel merkatoh* |

| Can I walk there? | Posso arrivarci a piedi? |
| | *possoh arreevarchee ah pyedee* |

CAR AND BIKE RENTAL

Where is the car rental desk?	Dov'è l'ufficio dell'autonoleggio? *doveh loofeechyo del owtonoledjoh*
I want to rent...	Vorrei noleggiare... *vorray noledjareh*
...a car	...un'automobile *oon owtomobeeleh*
...a bicycle	...una bicicletta *oonah beecheeklettah*
for...days	per...giorni *pehr...jornee*
for a week	per una settimana *pehr oonah setteemanah*

la berlina
lah berleenah
sedan

il portellone posteriore
eel portelloneh posteryoreh
hatchback

la motocicletta
lah motocheekletah
motorcycle

lo scooter
loh scooter
scooter

la bicicletta da strada
*lah beecheeklettah
dah stradah*
road bike

la mountain bike
lah mountain bike
mountain bike

for the weekend	per un fine settimana *pehr oon feeneh setteemanah*
I'd like...	Vorrei... *vorray*
...an automatic	...un'automobile con il cambio automatico *oon owtomobeeleh kon eel kambyo owtomateekoh*
...a manual	...un'automobile con il cambio manuale *oon owtomobeeleh kon eel kambyo manwaleh*
Here's my driver's license	Ecco la mia patente di guida *ekko lah mee-ah patenteh dee gweedah*
Can I hire a GPS receiver?	Posso noleggiare... *possoh noledjareh*
Do you have a...	Avete... *aveteh*

il casco
eel kaskoh
cycling helmet

il lucchetto
eel lookettoh
lock

il seggiolino per bambini
eel sedjoleenoh pehr bambeenee
child seat

GETTING AROUND

DRIVING

Is this the road to...?	È questa la strada per...? *eh kwestah lah stradah pehr*
Where is the nearest garage?	Qual è l'officina più vicina? *kwaleh lofeecheenah pew veecheenah*
I'd like...	Vorrei... *vorray*
...some gas	...del carburante *del karbooranteh*
...40 liters of unleaded	...quaranta litri di benzina senza piombo *kwarantah leetree dee bentseenah sentsah pyomboh*
...30 liters of diesel	...trenta litri di gasolio *trentah leetree dee gazolyo*
Fill it up, please	Il pieno, per favore *eel pyenoh, pehr favoreh*
Where do I pay?	Dove pago? *doveh pagoh*
The pump number is...	La pompa numero... *lah pompah noomeroh…*
Can I pay by credit card?	Posso pagare con la carta di credito? *possoh pagareh kon lah kartah dee kredeetoh*
Can you check...	Può controllare... *pwo kontrollareh*
...the oil	...l'olio *lolyo*
...the tire pressure	...la pressione dei pneumatici *lah pressyoneh day pneuhmateechee*

PARKING

Is there a parking lot nearby?	C'è un parcheggio nelle vicinanze? *che oon parkedjo nelleh veecheenantse*
Can I park here?	Posso parcheggiare qui? *possoh parkedjareh kwee*
Is it free?	È gratuito? *eh gratweetoh*
How much does it cost?	Quanto costa? *kwantoh kostah*
How much is it...	Quanto costa... *kwantoh kostah*
...per hour?	...all'ora? *alorah*
...per day?	...al giorno? *al jornoh*
...overnight?	...fino al giorno dopo? *feenoh al jornoh dopoh*

il portapacchi
eel portapakee
roofrack

il seggiolino
per bambini
*eel sedjoleenoh
pehr bambeenee*
child seat

la stazione di servizio
lah statsyoneh dee serveetsyo
gas station

THE CAR

il bagagliaio
eel bagalyayo
trunk

la marmitta
lah marmeetah
exhaust

la ruota
lah rwotah
wheel

lo sportello
loh sportelloh
door

INSIDE THE CAR

il poggiatesta
eel podjatestah
head rest

la maniglia
lah maneelya
handle

il sedile anteriore
eel sedeeleh anteryoreh
front seat

la chiusura
lah kewsoorah
door lock

la cintura
di sicurezza
*lah cheentoorah
dee seekooredza*
seat belt

il sedile
posteriore
*eel sedeeleh
posteryoreh*
back seat

il parabrezza
eel parabredza
windshield

il cofano
eel kofanoh
hood

i fari
ee faree
headlight

il pneumatico
eel pneoomateekoh
tire

il motore
eel motoreh
engine

il paraurti
eel parowrtee
bumper

MEGANE

THE CONTROLS

l'impiano stereo
leempyantoh stereo
car stereo

le frecce lampeggianti
leh fretcheh lampedjantee
hazard lights

il tachimetro
eel takeemetroh
speedometer

l'airbag
lairbag
airbag

il cruscotto
eel krooskottoh
dashboard

il clacson
eel klakson
horn

la leva del
cambio
*lah levah
del kambyo*
gear shift

lo sterzo
loh stertso
steering wheel

ROAD SIGNS

senso unico
senzoh ooneeko
one way

rotatoria
rotatorya
traffic circle

dare la precedenza
dareh lah prechedentsa
yield

divieto di sosta
deevyetoh dee sostah
no stopping

divieto di accesso
deevyetoh dee atchessoh
no entry

sosta vietata
sostah vyetatah
no parking

limite di velocità
leemeeteh dee velocheetah
speed limit

pericolo
pereekoloh
hazard

ON THE ROAD

il parchimetro
eel parkeemetroh
parking meter

il semaforo
eel semaforoh
traffic light

il vigile
eel veejeeleh
traffic police officer

l'attraversamento
pedonale
*latraversamentoh
pedonaleh*
pedestrian crossing

la cartina
lah karteenah
map

il parcheggio
per disabili
*eel parkedjoh pehr
deezabeelee*
disabled parking

l'autostrada
lowtostradah
highway

la bretella
lah bretellah
entrance/exit ramp

il telefono
d'emergenza
*eel telefonoh dee
emerjentsa*
emergency phone

AT THE STATION 🎧

Where can I buy a ticket?	Dove posso acquistare un biglietto? *doveh possoh akweestareh oon beelyettoh*
Is there an automatic ticket machine?	C'è una biglietteria automatica? *che oonah beelyettereeya owtomateekah*
Two tickets to...	Due biglietti per... *dooeh beelyettee pehr*
I'd like...	Vorrei... *vorray*
...a one-way ticket to...	...un biglietto di sola andata per... *oon beelyettoh dee solah andatah pehr*
...a return ticket to...	...un biglietto di andata e ritorno per... *oon beelyettoh dee andatah eh reetornoh pehr*
...a first-class ticket	...un biglietto di prima classe *oon beelyettoh dee preemah klasseh*
...a standard-class ticket	...un biglietto di classe economica *oon beelyettoh dee klasseh ekonomeekah*
Is it a fast/slow train?	È un treno rapido/locale? *eh oon trenoh rapeedoh/lokaleh*

il biglietto
eel beelyettoh
ticket

la biglietteria automatica
lah beelyetterya owtomateekah
automatic ticket machine

I'd like to...	Vorrei... *vorray*
...reserve a seat	...prenotare un posto *prenotareh oon postoh*
...on the Eurostar to...	...sull'Eurostar per... *soolehoorostar pehr*
...book a sleeper berth	...prenotare una cuccetta *prenotareh oonah koochettah*
Is there a reduction...	C'è una riduzione... *che oonah reedootsyoneh*
...for children?	...per i bambini? *pehr ee bambeenee*
...for students?	...per gli studenti? *pehr lyee stoodentee*
...for senior citizens?	...per gli anziani? *pehr lyee antsyanee*
Is there a dining car?	C'è una carrozza ristorante? *che oonah karrodza reestoranteh*
Do I stamp the ticket before boarding?	Devo vidimare il biglietto prima di salire in carrozza? *devoh veedeemareh eel beelyettoh preemah dee saleereh een karrodza*

YOU MAY HEAR...

Il treno parte dal binario...
eel trenoh parteh dal beenaryo
The train leaves from platform...

Deve cambiare treno
deveh kambyareh trenoh
You must change trains

TRAVELING BY TRAIN

Do you have a timetable?
Ha un orario?
ah oon oraryo

What time is...
A che ora è...
ah ke orah eh

...the next train to...?
...il prossimo treno per...?
eel prosseemoh trenoh pehr

...the last train to...?
...l'ultimo treno per...?
loolteemoh trenoh pehr

Which platform does it
leave from?
Da quale binario parte?
dah kwaleh beenaryo parteh

What time does it arrive in...?
A che ora arriva a...?
a ke orah arreevah ah

How long does it take?
Quanto tempo ci impiega?
kwantoh tempoh chee eempyegah

Is this the train for...?
È questo il treno per...?
eh kwestoh eel trenoh pehr

Is this the right platform for...?
È questo il binario giusto per...?
eh kwestoh eel beenaryo jewstoh pehr

Where is platform three?
Dov'è il binario tre?
doveh eel beenaryo treh

Does this train stop at...?
Questo treno ferma a...?
kwestoh trenoh fermah ah

YOU MAY HEAR...

Deve vidimare il biglietto
deveh veedeemareh eel beelyettoh
You must validate your ticket

Usi la macchinetta gialla
oozee lah makeenettah jallah
Use the yellow machine

Where do I change for...?	Dove devo cambiare per...? *doveh devoh kambyareh pehr*
Is this seat free?	È libero questo posto? *eh leeberoh kwestoh postoh*
I've reserved this seat	Ho prenotato questo posto *oh prenotatoh kwestoh postoh*
Do I get off here?	Devo scendere qui? *devoh shendereh kwee*
Where is the subway station?	Dov'è la stazione della metropolitana? *doveh lah statsyoneh dellah metropoleetanah*
Which line goes to...?	Quale linea arriva a...? *kwaleh leeneah arrivah ah*
How many stops is it?	Quante fermate sono? *kwanteh fermateh sonoh*

l'atrio
latryo
concourse

il treno
eel trenoh
train

la carrozza
ristorante
*lah karrodzah
reestoranteh*
dining car

la cuccetta
lah kootchettah
sleeper berth

BUSES

When is the next bus to...?	Quando parte il prossimo autobus per...? *kwandoh parteh eel prosseemoh owtoboos pehr*
What is the fare to...?	Quanto costa un biglietto per...? *kwantoh kostah oon beelyettoh pehr*
Where is the bus stop?	Dov'è la fermata dell'autobus? *doveh lah fermatah del owtoboos*
Is this the bus stop for...?	È questa la fermata dell'autobus per...? *eh kwestah lah fermatah del owtoboos pehr*
Where can I buy a ticket?	Dove posso acquistare un biglietto? *doveh possoh akweestareh oon beelyettoh*
Can I pay on the bus?	Posso pagare sull'autobus? *possoh pagareh soolowtoboos*
Which buses go to the city center?	Quali autobus raggiungono il centro? *kwalee owtoboos radjewngonoh eel chentroh*
Will you tell me when to get off?	Mi può dire quando devo scendere? *mee pwo deereh kwandoh devoh shendereh*

l'autobus
lowtoboos
bus

la stazione degli autobus
lah statsyoneh delyee owtoboos
bus station

TAXIS

Can I order a taxi?	Dove posso richiedere un taxi? *doveh possoh reekyedereh oon taxi*
I want a taxi to...	Desidero un taxi per... *deseederoh oon taxi pehr*
Can you take me to...?	Mi può portare a/in...? *mee pwo portareh ah/een*
Is it far?	È lontano? *eh lontanoh*
How much will it cost?	Quanto costa? *kwantoh kostah*
Can you drop me here?	Mi può far scendere qui? *mee pwo far shendereh kwee*
What do I owe you?	Quanto le devo? *kwantoh leh devoh*
I don't have any change	Non ho spiccioli *non oh speetchyolee*
Keep the change	Tenga il resto *tengah eel restoh*
Please may I have a receipt	Potrei avere la ricevuta, per favore *potray avereh lah reechevootah pehr favoreh*
Please wait for me	Mi aspetti, per favore *mee aspeteeh pehr favoreh*

il taxi
eel taxee
taxi

BOATS 🎧

Are there any boat trips?	Ci sono navi in partenza? *chee sonoh navee een partentsa*
Where does the boat leave from?	Dove parte la nave? *doveh parteh lah naveh*
When is...	Quando parte... *kwandoh parteh*
...the next boat to...?	...la prossima nave per...? *lah prosseemah naveh pehr*
...the first boat?	...la prima nave? *lah preemah naveh*
...the last boat?	...l'ultima nave? *loolteemah naveh*
I'd like two tickets for...	Vorrei due biglietti per... *vorray dooeh beelyettee pehr*
...the cruise	...la crociera *lah crotchyerah*

il traghetto
eel tragettoh
ferry

l'aliscafo
laleeskafoh
hydrofoil

la barca
a vela
*lah barka
ah velah*
yacht

l'hovercraft
lovercraft
hovercraft

...the river trip
...la gita sul fiume
lah jeetah sool fewmeh

How much is it for...
Quanto costa per...
kwantoh kostah pehr

...a car and two people?
...un'automobile e due persone?
oon owtomobeeleh eh dooeh personeh

...a family?
...una famiglia?
oona fameelyah

...a cabin?
...una cabina?
oonah kabeenah

Can I buy a ticket
on board?
Posso acquistare il biglietto
a bordo?
*possoh akweestareh eel beelyettoh
ah bordoh*

Is there wheelchair
access?
C'è un accesso per disabili?
che oon atchessoh pehr deezabeelee

ll motoscafo
eel motoscarfoh
motorboat

il salvagente
eel salvajenteh
life ring

il catamarano
eel katamaranoh
catamaran

il giubbotto di
salvataggio
*eel jewbottoh
dee salvatadjoh*
life jacket

AIR TRAVEL

Which terminal do I need?	A quale terminal devo andare? *ah kwaleh terminahl devoh andareh*
Where do I check in?	Dove posso effettuare il check-in? *doveh possoh effetwareh eel check-in*
Where is...	Dove si trovano... *doveh see trovanoh*
...the arrivals hall?	...gli arrivi? *lyee arreevee*
...the departures hall?	...le partenze? *leh partentse*
...the boarding gate?	...le uscite d'imbarco? *leh oosheeteh deembarkoh*
I'm traveling...	Viaggio... *vyadjoh*
...economy	...in classe economica *een klasseh ekonomeeka*
...business class	... in business class *een business class*

la sacca da viaggio
lah sakah dah vyadjo
duffel bag

il passaporto
eel passaportoh
passport

il pasto a bordo
*eel pastoh
ah bordoh*
in-flight meal

la carta
d'imbarco
*lah kartah
deembarko*
boarding pass

I'm checking in one suitcase	Desidero imbarcare un bagaglio *deseederoh eembarkareh oon bagalyo*
I packed it myself	Ho preparato io il bagaglio *oh preparatoh eeoh eel bagalyo*
I have one piece of hand luggage	Ho un unico bagaglio a mano *oh oon ooneeko bagalyo ah manoh*
How much is excess baggage?	A quanto ammonta il peso in eccesso? *ah kwantoh amontah eel pezoh een etchessoh*
Will a meal be served?	Sarà servito un pasto? *sarah serveetoh oon pastoh*
I'd like...	Vorrei... *vorray*
...a window seat	...un posto vicino al finestrino *oon postoh veecheenoh al feenestreenoh*
...an aisle seat	...un posto vicino al corridoio *oon postoh veecheenoh al koreedoyo*

YOU MAY HEAR...

Il suo passaporto/biglietto, per favore
eel soowo passaportoh/ beelyettoh pehr favoreh
Your passport/ticket, please

È sua questa borsa?
eh soowa kwestah borsah
Is this your bag?

AT THE AIRPORT

Here's my...	Ecco... *ekko*
...boarding pass	...la mia carta d'imbarco *la meeah karta deembarkoh*
...passport	...il mio passaporto *eel meeoh passaportoh*
Can I change some money?	Potrei cambiare del denaro? *potray kambyareh dehl denaroh?*
What is the exchange rate?	Qual è il tasso di cambio? *kwaleh eel tassoh dee kambyo*
Is the flight delayed?	Il volo è in ritardo? *eel voloh eh een reetardoh*

banco del check-in
banko del chek een
check-in

ufficio di cambio
oofeechyo dee kambyo
currency exchange booth

il controllo passaporti
eel kontrolloh passaportee
passport control

il negozio duty-free
eel negotsyo dootee free
duty-free shop

il ritiro bagagli
eel reeteeroh bagalyee
baggage claim

il pilota
eel peelotah
pilot

l'aeroplano
lahehroplahnoh
airplane

l'assistente di volo
lasseestenteh dee voloh
flight attendant

How late is it?	Quanto porta di ritardo? *kwantoh portah dee reetardoh*
Which gate does flight... leave from?	Qual è l'uscita del volo...? *kwaleh loosheetah del voloh*
What time do I board?	A che ora ci imbarchiamo? *ah keh orah chee eembarkyamoh*
When does the gate close?	Quando chiude l'uscita d'imbarco? *kwandoh kewdeh loosheetah deembarkoh*
Where are the carts?	Dove sono i carrelli? *doveh sonoh ee karrelee*
Here is the baggage claim tag	Ecco la ricevuta dei bagagli *ekko lah reechevootah day bagalye*
I can't find my baggage	Non trovo i miei bagagli *non trovoh ee myayee bagalye*

EATING OUT

It is not difficult to eat well and inexpensively in Italy. You can choose from cafés and bars, which serve a variety of drinks, snacks, and light meals, *osterie* and *trattorie* (small family-run restaurants which serve local and traditional dishes), and *pizzerie* (for pizzas and pasta). If you want a gastronomic meal in more formal surroundings, you can eat at more expensive *ristorante* but you may have to book in advance at the popular ones.

MAKING A RESERVATION

I'd like to book a table...	Vorrei prenotare un tavolo... *voray prenotareh oon tavoloh*
...for lunch/dinner	...per pranzo/cena *pehr prandzo/ chenah*
...for four people	...per quattro persone *pehr kwatroh personeh*
...for this evening	...per questa sera *pehr kwestah serah*
...for tomorrow at one	...per l'una di domani *pehr loonah dee domanee*
...for today	...per oggi *pehr odjee*
Do you have a table earlier/later?	Ha un tavolo prima/più tardi? *ah oon tavoloh preemah/pew tardee*
My name is...	Il cognome è... *eel konyomeh eh*
My telephone number is...	Il mio numero di telefono è... *eel meeoh noomeroh dee telefonoh eh*
Do you take credit cards?	Accettate carte di credito? *atchettateh karteh dee kredeetoh*
I have a reservation	Ho una prenotazione *oh oonah prenotatsyoneh*
in the name of...	a nome di... *ah nomeh dee*
We haven't booked	Non abbiamo prenotato *non abyamoh prenotatoh*
May we sit here?	Possiamo sederci qui? *possyamoh sederchee kwee*
We'd like to eat outside	Vorremmo mangiare fuori *vorremoh manjareh fworee*

ORDERING A MEAL

May we see the menu?	Possiamo vedere il menù? *possyamoh vedereh eel menoo*
...the wine list?	...la carta dei vini? *lah kartah day veenee*
Do you have...	Ha... *ah*
...a set menu?	...un menù fisso? *oon menoo feesoh*
...a fixed-price menu?	...un menù a prezzo fisso? *oon menoo ah predzo feesoh*
...a children's menu?	...un menù per bambini? *oon menoo pehr bambeenee*
...an à la carte menu	...un menù alla carta? *oon menoo allah kartah*
What are today's specials?	Qual è la specialità del giorno? *kwaleh lah spechyaleetah del jornoh*
What is this?	Cos'è questo/a? *kozeh kwestoh/ah*

YOU MAY HEAR...

Ha prenotato?
ah prenotatoh
Do you have a reservation?

Si sieda per favore
see syedah pehr favoreh
Please be seated

A nome di?
ah nomeh dee
In what name?

Vuole ordinare?
vwoleh ordeenareh
Are you ready to order?

Are there any vegetarian dishes?	Avete dei piatti vegetariani? *aveteh day pyatee vejetaryanee*
I can't eat...	Non posso mangiare... *non possoh manjareh*
...dairy foods	...i latticini *ee latteecheenee*
...nuts	...la frutta secca *lah frootah sekah*
...wheat	...il frumento *eel froomentoh*
To drink, I'll have...	Da bere, vorrei... *dah bereh vorray*
May we have...	Possiamo avere... *possyamoh avereh*
...some water	...dell'acqua? *delakwa*
...some bread?	...del pane? *del paneh*
...the dessert menu?	...il menù dei dolci? *eel menoo day dolchee*

READING THE MENU...

gli antipasti *lyee anteepastee* **appetizers**	i secondi *ee sekondee* **main courses**	i formaggi *ee formadjee* **cheeses**
i primi *ee preemee* **first courses**	i contorni *ee kontornee* **vegetables**	i dolci *ee dolchee* **desserts**

COMPLAINING

I didn't order this
Non ho ordinato questo/a
non oh ordeenatoh kwestoh/ah

When is our food coming?
Quando arriva il cibo?
kwandoh arreevah eel cheeboh

We can't wait any longer
Non possiamo aspettare oltre
non possyamoh aspettareh oltreh

PAYING

The check, please
Il conto, per favore
eel kontoh pehr favoreh

Can we pay separately?
Possiamo pagare separatamente?
possyamoh pagareh separatamenteh

May I have...
Posso avere...
possoh avereh

...a receipt?
...la ricevuta?
lah reechevootah

...an itemized bill?
...una ricevuta dettagliata?
*oonah reechevootah
detalyatah*

Is service included?
Il servizio è incluso?
*eel serveetsyo eh
eenkloozoh*

YOU MAY HEAR...

Non accettiamo carte di credito
non atchetyamoh karteh dee kredeetoh
We don't take credit cards

Digiti il PIN
deejeetee eel peen
Please enter your PIN

DISHES AND CUTLERY

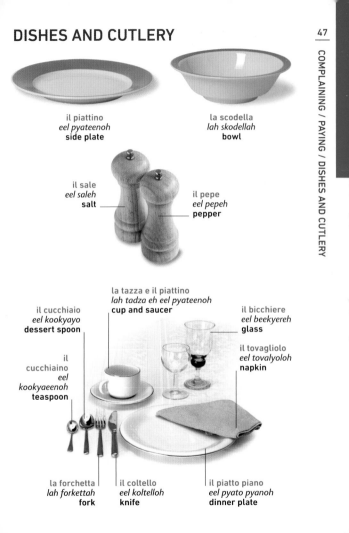

il piattino
eel pyateenoh
side plate

la scodella
lah skodellah
bowl

il sale
eel saleh
salt

il pepe
eel pepeh
pepper

il cucchiaio
eel kookyayo
dessert spoon

la tazza e il piattino
lah tadza eh eel pyateenoh
cup and saucer

il bicchiere
eel beekyereh
glass

il tovagliolo
eel tovalyoloh
napkin

il cucchiaino
eel kookyaeenoh
teaspoon

la forchetta
lah forkettah
fork

il coltello
eel koltelloh
knife

il piatto piano
eel pyato pyanoh
dinner plate

AT THE CAFÉ OR BAR

The menu, please	Il menù, per favore *eel menooh pehr favoreh*
Do you have...?	Ha...? *ah*
What fruit juices/herbal teas do you have?	Quali succhi di frutta/tisane ha? *kwalee sookee dee frootah/teezaneh ah*
I'd like...	Vorrei... *juh vorray*

un caffellatte
oon kaffelatteh
coffee with milk

un caffè
oon kaffeh
black coffee

un espresso
oon espressoh
espresso

un cappuccino
oon kapootcheenoh
cappuccino

YOU MAY HEAR...

Cosa desidera?
kozah deseederah
What would you like?

Altro?
altroh
Anything else?

Prego
pregoh
You're welcome

un tè al latte
oon teh al latteh
tea with milk

un tè al limone
oon teh al leemoneh
tea with lemon

un tè alla menta
oon teh allah mentah
mint tea

un tè verde
oon teh verdeh
green tea

una camomilla
oonah kamomeelah
chamomile tea

una cioccolata calda
oonah chokolatah kaldah
hot chocolate

A bottle of...	Una bottiglia di... *oonah botteelya dee*
A glass of...	Un bicchiere di... *oon beekyereh dee*
A cup of...	Una tazza di... *oonah tadza dee*
With lemon/milk	Con limone/latte *kon leemoneh/latteh*
Another...please	Un altro/a...per favore *oon altroh/ah...pehr favoreh*
The same again, please	Me ne porta ancora, per favore *meh neh portah ankorah pehr favoreh*

CAFÉ AND BAR DRINKS 🎧

un succo di ananas
oon sookoh dee ananas
pineapple juice

un succo di mela
oon sookoh dee melah
apple juice

una spremuta d'arancia
oonah spremootah daranchya
fresh orange juice

una limonata
oonah leemonatah
lemonade

un succo d'uva
oon sookoh doovah
grape juice

un succo di pomodoro
oon sookoh dee pomodoroh
tomato juice

un crodino
oon krodeenoh
Crodino

una coca cola
oonah kokakolah
cola

un caffè shakerato
oon kaffeh shakeratoh
iced coffee

un campari
oon kamparee
Campari

una grappa
oonah grappah
Grappa

una birra
oonah beerrah
beer

acqua minerale
akwa meeneraleh
mineral water

un prosecco
oon prosekoh
sparkling wine

un vino bianco
oon veenoh byankoh
white wine

un vino rosso
oon veenoh rossoh
red wine

YOU MAY HEAR...

In bottiglia o alla spina?
een botteelya oh allah speenah
Bottled or draft?

Liscia o gassata?
leesha oh gassatah
Still or sparkling?

Con ghiaccio?
kon gyachyo
With ice?

BAR SNACKS

un tramezzino
oon tramedzeenoh
sandwich

un panino
oon paneenoh
panino

le olive
leh oliveh
olives

le nocciloine
leh notcholeeneh
nuts

il condimento
eel kondimentoh
dressing

l'insalata
leensalatah
salad

i biscotti
ee beeskottee
biscotti

la bruschetta
lah brooskettah
bruschetta

il gelato
eel jelatoh
ice cream

i maritozzi
ee mareetodzee
cream buns

FAST FOOD

May I have...

Posso avere...
possoh avereh

...to eat in/carry out

...da mangiare qui/da portare via
dah manjareh kwee/dah portareh vee-ah

un hamburger
oon amboorger
hamburger

un hamburger
di pollo
*oon amboorger
dee polloh*
chicken burger

una piadina
arrotolata
*oonah pyadeenah
arotolatah*
wrap

un hot dog
oon otdog
hot dog

un kebab
oon kebab
kebab

le patatine
leh patateeneh
French fries

il pollo fritto
eel polloh freetoh
fried chicken

la pizza
lah peedza
pizza

BREAKFAST

May I have...	Posso avere... *possoh avereh*
...some milk	...del latte? *del latteh*
...some sugar	dello zucchero? *delloh tsookeroh*
...some artificial sweetener	...del dolcificante? *del dolcheefeekanteh*
...some butter	...del burro? *del booroh*
...some jam?	...della marmellata? *dellah marmellatah*
...some salt/pepper?	...del sale/del pepe? *del saleh/del pehpeh*

un caffè
oon kaffeh
coffee

un tè
oon teh
tea

una cioccolata
calda
*oonah
chokolatah
kaldah*
hot chocolate

una spremuta
d'arancia
*oonah
spremootah
daranchya*
orange juice

un succo di mela
*oon sookoh dee
melah*
apple juice

il pane
eel paneh
bread

un panino
oon paneenoh
bread roll

il miele
eel myeleh
honey

un cornetto
oon kornettoh
croissant

la marmellata
lah marmellatah
marmalade

un cornetto al
cioccolato
*oon kornettoh
al chokolatoh*
**chocolate
croissant**

le uova
strapazzate
*leh wovah
strapadzateh*
**scrambled
eggs**

l'uovo sodo
lwovoh sodoh
boiled egg

l'uovo in camicia
*lwovoh een
kameecha*
poached egg

lo yoghurt
alla frutta
*loh yogoort
allah frootah*
fruit yogurt

la frutta fresca
*lah frootah
freskah*
fresh fruit

FIRST COURSES

la minestra
lah meenestrah
soup

il brodo
eel brodoh
broth

la zuppa di
pesce
*lah tsoopah dee
pesheh*
fish soup

il minestrone
*eel
meenestroneh*
minestrone

il prosciutto
crudo
*eel proshewtoh
kroodoh*

i gamberi alla
griglia
*ee gamberee
allah greelya*

la bresaola
lah bresaolah
bresaola

il risotto
eel reezottoh
risotto

gli gnocchi
lyee nyokee
gnocchi

i tortelloni
ee tortellonee
tortelloni

le sarde al saor
leh sardeh al saor
**Venetian-style
sardines**

gli spaghetti
alla bolognese
*lyee spagetee
alla bolonyeseh*
**spaghetti
bolognese**

gli spaghetti
alla vongole
*lyee spagetee
alla vongoleh*
**spaghetti
with clams**

gli spaghetti
alla carbonara
*lyee spagetee
alla karbonara*
**spaghetti
carbonara**

l'antipasto misto
*lanteepastoh
meestoh*
mixed antipasto

i cannelloni
ee kannellonee
cannelloni

la frittata
lah freetatah
omelet

l'antipasto freddo
*lanteepastoh
freddoh*
**antipasto of
cold meats**

la bagna cauda
*lah banya
cowdah*
**hot anchovy
dip**

l'antipasto
di mare
*lanteepastoh
dee mareh*
**seafood
antipasto**

MAIN COURSES

I would like...	Vorrei... *vorray*	...the liver	...il fegato *eel fegatoh*
...the chicken	...il pollo *eel polloh*	roast	arrosto *arrostoh*
...the duck	...l'anatra *lanatrah*	baked	al forno *al fornoh*
...the lamb	...l'agnello *lanyelloh*	broiled	alla griglia *allah greelya*
...the pork	...il maiale *eel mayaleh*	on skewers	allo spiedo *alloh spyedoh*
...the beef	...il manzo *eel mandzo*	barbecued	al barbecue *al barbekew*
...the steak	...la bistecca *lah beestekkah*	poached	in camicia *een kameechya*
...the veal	...il vitello *eel veeteloh*	boiled	lesso/sodo *lessoh/sodoh*

YOU MAY SEE...

i frutti di mare
ee frootee dee mareh
seafood

il pesce
eel pesheh
fish

YOU MAY HEAR...

Come desidera la bistecca?
komeh deseederah lah beestekkah
How do you like your steak?

Al sangue, a cottura
media o ben cotta?
*al sangweh, ah kottoorah medya
oh ben kottah*
Rare, medium rare, or well done?

fried	fritto *freetoh*	**stewed**	stufato *stoofatoh*
pan-fried/ sautéed	in padella/saltato *een padellah/saltatoh*	**...with Parmesan cheese**	...con il parmigiano *kon eel parmeejanoh*
stuffed	farcito *farcheetoh*		

il pollame
eel pollameh
poultry

la carne
lah karneh
meat

SALADS AND SIDE DISHES

l'insalata
verde
*leensalatah
verdeh*
green salad

l'insalata mista
*leensalatah
meestah*
mixed salad

il radicchio
alla griglia
*eel radeekkyo
allah greelya*
grilled radicchio

gli asparagi
lyee asparajee
asparagus

gli spinaci
*lyee
speenachee*
spinach

le verdure
al vapore
*leh verdooreh
al vaporeh*
**steamed
vegetables**

le patatine
fritte
*leh patateeneh
freeteh*
French fries

la pasta
lah pastah
pasta

la polenta
lah polentah
polenta

il riso
eel reezoh
rice

DESSERTS

lo zabaglione
loh tsabalyoneh
zabaglione

il gelato
eel jelatoh
ice cream

la mousse di
cioccolato
*lah moos dee
chokolatoh*
**chocolate
mousse**

la crostata
di frutta
*lah krostatah
dee frootah*
fruit tart

la cassata
lah kassatah
cassata

il tiramisù
eel teerameesoo
tiramisù

il sorbetto
eel sorbettoh
sherbet

la torta
lah tortah
cake

la crostata di
ricotta
*lah krostatah
dee reekottah*
ricotta tart

la crostata di
nocciole
*lah krostatah
dee nochyoleh*
hazelnut tart

PLACES TO STAY

Italy has a wide range of places to stay, depending on your personal preference and budget. These range from elegant hotels in former *palazzi* to smaller *alberghi*, *locande* (one-star hotels), and family-run *pensioni*. If you want a self-catering option, however, you can choose to rent a seaside apartment or a country villa, or find a campsite to park your camper van or put up your tent.

MAKING A RESERVATION

I'd like...	Vorrei... *vorray*
...to make a reservation	...fare una prenotazione *fareh oonah prenotatsyoneh*
...a double room	...una camera doppia *oonah kamerah doppya*
...a room with two twin beds	...una camera a due letti *oonah kamerah ah dooeh lettee*
...a single room	...una camera singola *oonah kamerah seengolah*
...a family room	...una camera familiare *oonah kamerah fameelyareh*
...a disabled person's room	...una camera per disabili *oonah kamerah pehr deezabeelee*
...with a bathtub/shower	...con bagno/doccia *kon banyo/dotchya*
...with a sea view	...con vista sul mare *kon veestah sool mareh*
...with a balcony	...con balcone *kon balkoneh*
...for two nights	...per due notti *pehr dooeh nottee*
...for a week	...per una settimana *pehr oonah setteemanah*
Is breakfast included?	La colazione è inclusa? *lah kolatsyoneh eh eenkloosah*
How much is it...	Quanto costa... *kwantoh kostah*
...per night?	...a notte? *ah notteh*
...per week?	...alla settimana? *allah setteemanah*

CHECKING IN

I have a reservation in the name of...
Ho una prenotazione a nome di...
oh oonah prenotatsyoneh ah nomeh dee

Do you have...
Ha...
ah

I'd like...
Vorrei...
vorray

...the keys for room...
...le chiavi della camera...
leh kyavee dellah kamerah

...a wake-up call at...
...la sveglia alle...
lah svelya alleh

What time is...
A che ora servite...
ah ke orah serveeteh

...breakfast?
...la colazione?
lah kolatsyoneh

...dinner?
...la cena?
lah chenah

un facchino
oon fakeenoh
porter

il mini bar
eel meenee bar
mini bar

il servizio in camera
eel serveetsyo een kamerah
room service

gli ascensori
lyee ashensoree
elevator

IN YOUR ROOM

Do you have...	Ha... *ah*
another...	un altro/a... *oon altroh/ah*
some more...	altri/e... *altree/eh*
I've lost my key	Ho perso la mia chiave *oh persoh lah meeah kiaveh*

le coperte
leh koperteh
blankets

i cuscini
ee koosheenee
pillows

un adattatore
oon adatatoreh
adapter

una lampadina
oonah lampadeenah
light bulb

YOU MAY HEAR...

Il suo numero di camera è...
eel soo-oh noomeroh dee kamerah eh
Your room number is...

Ecco la sua chiave
ekko lah sooah kiaveh
Here is your key

IN THE HOTEL

The room is...	La camera è... *lah kamerah e*
...too hot	...troppo calda *troppoh kaldah*
...too cold	...troppo fredda *troppoh freddah*
...too small	...troppo piccola *troppoh peekolah*
The window won't open	La finestra non si apre *lah feenestrah non see apreh*
The TV doesn't work	Il televisore non funziona *eel televeezoreh non funtsyonah*

il bollitore
eel bolleetoreh
kettle

il radiatore
eel radyatoreh
radiator

il termostato
eel termostatoh
thermostat

la camera singola
lah kamerah seengolah
single room

la camera doppia
lah kamerah doppya
double room

il numero della camera
eel noomeroh dellah kamerah
room number

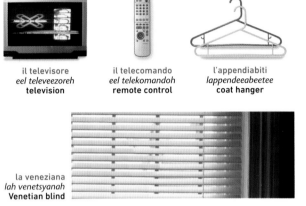

il televisore
eel televeezoreh
television

il telecomando
eel telekomandoh
remote control

l'appendiabiti
lappendeeabeetee
coat hanger

la veneziana
lah venetsyanah
Venetian blind

CHECKING OUT

When do I have to vacate the room?	Quando devo lasciare la stanza? *kwandoh devoh lasheeareh lah standza*
Is there a porter to carry my bags?	C'è un facchino per portare le mie valigie? *che oon fakkeenoh pehr portareh leh meeye valeejeh*
May I have the bill, please?	Posso avere il conto? *possoh avereh eel kontoh*
Can I pay...	Posso pagare... *possoh pagareh*
...by credit card?	...con la carta di credito? *kon lah kartah dee kredeetoh*
...cash?	...in contanti? *een kontantee*
I'd like a receipt	Vorrei la ricevuta *vorray lah reechevootah*

IN THE BATHROOM

gli asciugamani
lyee ashewgamanee
towels

l'accappatoio
lakappatoyo
bathrobe

il sapone
eel saponeh
soap

il deodorante
eel dehodoranteh
deodorant

il dentifricio
eel denteefreechyo
toothpaste

il bagnoschiuma
eel banyoskewmah
bubblebath

il bidet
eel beedeh
bidet

il docciaschiuma
eel dotchyaskwemah
shower gel

la vasca
da bagno
*lah vaska
dah banyo*
bathtub

la crema
per il corpo
*lah kremah
pehr eel korpoh*
body lotion

lo spazzolino da denti
*loh spatsoleenoh
dah dentee*
toothbrush

l'asciugacapelli
lashewgakapellee
blow-dryer

il rasoio elettrico
eel rasoyo eletreeko
electric razor

la schiuma
da barba
*lah skewmah
dah barbah*
shaving foam

il rasoio
eel rasoyo
razor

il colluttorio
eel kolootoryo
mouthwash

lo shampoo
loh shampoh
shampoo

il balsamo
eel balsamoh
conditioner

il tagliaunghie
eel talyaoongye
nail clippers

le forbici
per unghie
*leh forbeechee
pehr oongye*
nail scissors

SELF-CATERING 🎧

May we have...	Possiamo avere... *possyamoh avereh*
...the key, please?	...la chiave, per favore? *lah kiaveh pehr favoreh*
...an extra bed?	...un letto extra? *oon lettoh extrah*
...a child's bed?	...un lettino? *oon letteenoh*
...more cutlery/ dishes	...più posate/stoviglie *pew posateh/stoveelye*
Where is...	Dov'è... *doveh*
...the fusebox?	...la scatola dei fusibili? *lah skatolah day fooseebeelee*
...the water valve?	...il rubinetto d'arresto? *eel roobeenettoh darrestoh*

il termoconvettore
eel termokonverteetoreh
space heater

il ventilatore
eel venteelatoreh
fan

il lettino
eel leteenoh
crib

il seggiolone
eel sedjoloneh
high chair

...the nearest store?	...il negozio più vicino? *eel negotsyo pew veecheenoh*
Do you do babysitting?	Offrite un servizio di babysitting? *offreeteh oon serveetsyo dee babyseetteeng*
How does the heating work?	Come funziona il riscaldamento? *komeh foontsyonah eel reeskaldamentoh*
Is there...	C'è... *che*
...air-conditioning?	...l'aria condizionata? *larya kondeetsyonatah*
...central heating?	...il riscaldamento centralizzato? *eel reeskaldamentoh chentraleedzatoh*
When does the cleaner come?	Quando passa l'addetto alle pulizie? *kwandoh passah ladettoh alleh pooleetsye*
Where do I put the garbage?	Dove posso buttare l'immondizia? *doveh possoh bootareh leemondeetsyah*
Do you allow pets?	Accettate animali domestici? *atchettateh aneemalee domesteechee*

il cane
eel kaneh
dog

IN THE VILLA

Is there an inventory?	C'è un inventario? *che oon eenventaryo*
Where is this item?	Dove si trova questo articolo? *doveh see trovah kwestoh arteekoloh*
I need...	Ho bisogno di... *oh beezonyo dee*
...an extension cord	...una prolunga *oonah proloongah*
...a flashlight	...una torcia *oonah torchya*
...matches	...dei fiammiferi *day fyameeferee*

il forno a microonde
eel fornoh ah meekrohondeh
microwave

il ferro da stiro
eel ferroh dah steeroh
iron

l'asse da stiro
lasseh dah steeroh
ironing board

il mocio e il secchio
eel mochyo eh
eel sekkyo
mop and bucket

la paletta e la scopetta
lah palettah eh
lah skopettah
dustpan and bush

il detersivo
eel deterseevoh
detergent

PROBLEM SOLVING

The shower doesn't work   La doccia non funziona
lah dotchya non foontsyonah

The toilet is leaking   Il water perde acqua
eel vater perdeh akwa

Can you fix it today?   Può aggiustarlo oggi?
pwo adjewstarloh odjee

There's no...   Non c'è...
non che

...electricity/gas   ...elettricità/gas
eletreecheetah/gas

...water   ...acqua
akwa

la lavatrice
lah lavatreeche
washing machine

il frigorifero
eel freegoreeferoh
refrigerator

l'estintore
lesteentoreh
fire extinguisher

il lucchetto e la chiave
*eel lookettoh
eh lah kiaveh*
lock and key

il rivelatore di fumo
*eel reevelatoreh
dee foomoh*
smoke alarm

la pattumiera
lah patoomyerah
trash can

KITCHEN EQUIPMENT

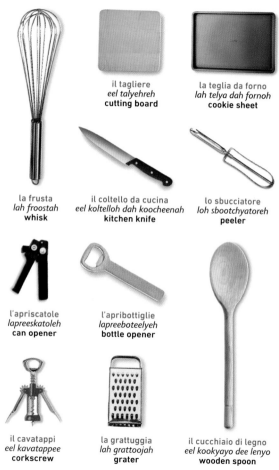

il tagliere
eel talyehreh
cutting board

la teglia da forno
lah telya dah fornoh
cookie sheet

la frusta
lah froostah
whisk

il coltello da cucina
eel koltelloh dah koocheenah
kitchen knife

lo sbucciatore
loh sbootchyatoreh
peeler

l'apriscatole
lapreeskatoleh
can opener

l'apribottiglie
lapreeboteelyeh
bottle opener

il cavatappi
eel kavatappee
corkscrew

la grattuggia
lah grattoojah
grater

il cucchiaio di legno
eel kookyayo dee lenyo
wooden spoon

la padella
lah padellah
frying pan

il colapasta
eel kolapastah
colander

la spatola
lah spatolah
spatula

la pentola
la pentolah
saucepan

la griglia
lah greelya
griddle pan

la casseruola
lah kasserwolah
casserole dish

l'insalatiera
leensalatyerah
mixing bowl

il grembiule
eel grembewleh
apron

i guanti da forno
ee gwantee dah fornoh
oven mitts

il frullatore
eel froolatoreh
blender

CAMPING

Where is the nearest...	Dov'è il più vicino... *doveh eel pew veecheenoh*
...campsite?	...campeggio? *kampedjoh*
...camper van site?	...campeggio per camper? *kampedjoh pehr kamper*
Can we camp here?	Possiamo accamparci qui? *possyamoh akamparchee kwee*
Do you have any vacancies?	C'è posto disponibile? *che postoh deesponeebeeleh*
What is the charge...	Quanto costa... *kwantoh kostah*
...per night?	...per notte? *pehr notteh*
...per week?	...per settimana? *pehr setteemanah*
Does the price include...	Il costo include... *eel kostoh eenkloodeh*
...electricity?	...l'elettricità? *leletreecheetah*
...hot water?	...l'acqua calda? *lakwa kaldah*
We want to stay for...	Desideriamo rimanere per... *deseederyamoh reemanereh pehr*

la tenda
lah tendah
tent

la corda
lah kordah
guy rope

il picchetto
eel peekkettoh
tent peg

Can I rent...	Posso noleggiare... *possoh noledjareh*
...a tent?	...una tenda? *oonah tendah*
...a barbecue?	...un barbecue? *oon barbecue*
Where are...	Dove sono... *doveh sonoh*
...the restrooms?	...i servizi? *ee serveetsee*
...the garbage cans?	...i bidoni dell'immondizia? *ee beedonee del eemondeetsya*
Are there...	Ci sono... *chee sonoh*
...showers?	...docce? *dotcheh*
...laundry facilities?	...servizi di lavanderia? *serveetsee dee lavanderya*
Is there...	C'è... *che*
...a swimming pool?	...una piscina? *oonah peesheenah*
...a store?	...un negozio? *oon negotsyo*

YOU MAY HEAR...

Non accendere il fuoco
non atchendereh eel fwoko
Don't light a fire

Non bere l'acqua
non bereh lakwa
Don't drink the water

AT THE CAMPSITE

il bollitore
eel boleetoreh
camping kettle

il thermos
eel termos
vacuum flask

il barbecue
eel barbecue
barbecue

il fornello da campeggio
eel fornelloh dah kampedjoh
camping stove

l'acqua in bottiglia
lakwa een botteelya
bottled water

il frigo portatile
eel freegoh portateeleh
cooler

il sacco a pelo
eel sakko ah peloh
sleeping bag

il materasso gonfiabile
eel materassoh gonfyabeeleh
air mattress

la torcia
lah torchya
flashlight

lo zaino
loh dzaeenoh
backpack

il secchio
eel sekyo
bucket

il maglio
eel malyo
mallet

il cestino da picnic
*eel chesteenoh
dah picnic*
picnic basket

il filtro solare
eel feeltroh solareh
sunscreen

i cerotti
ee cherotee
**adhesive
bandage**

la matassa
di spago
*lah matassah
dee spagoh*
ball of string

gli scarponi
da montagna
*lye skarponee
dah montanya*
hiking boots

la bussola
lah boosolah
compass

SHOPPING

As well as shopping malls, supermarkets, and specialist shops, Italy has many picturesque open-air markets in town squares and on high streets where you can buy food, clothes, and even antiques relatively cheaply. Most shops are open between 8.30am and 12.30pm, and 3.30pm to 7.30pm from Tuesday to Saturday. Be aware that many stores and food shops are shut on Monday mornings or all day Mondays.

IN THE STORE

I'm looking for...
Sto cercando...
stoh cherkandoh

Do you have...?
Avete...?
aveteh

I'm just looking
Sto solo guardando
stoh soloh gwardandoh

I'm being served
Mi stanno già servendo
mee stannoh jah servendoh

Do you have any more of these?
Ne avete ancora?
eh aveteh ankorah

How much is this?
Quanto costa questo?
wantoh kostah kwestoh

Have you anything cheaper?
Avete qualcosa di
meno costoso?
*aveteh kwalkosah dee
menoh kostosoh*

I'll take this one
Prendo questo/a
prendoh kwestoh/ah

Where can I pay?
Dove posso pagare?
doveh possoh pagareh

I'll pay...
Desidero pagare...
deseederoh pagareh

...in cash
...in contanti
een kontantee

...by credit card
...con la carta di credito
kon lah kartah dee kredeetoh

May I have a receipt?
Mi può fare lo scontrino?
mee pwo fareh loh skontreenoh

I'd like to exchange this
Vorrei cambiare questo/a
vorray kambyareh kwestoh/ah

IN THE BANK

I'd like...	Desidero... *deseederoh*
...to make a withdrawal	...effettuare un prelievo *effettwareh oon prelyevoh*
...to deposit some money	...effettuare un deposito *effettwareh oon deposeetoh*
...to change some money	...cambiare del denaro *kambyareh del denaroh*
...into euros	...in euro *een ehooroh*
...into dollars/sterling	...in dollari/sterline *een dohlaree/sterleeneh*
Here is my passport	Ecco il mio passaporto *ekko eel meeo passaportoh*
My name is...	Mi chiamo... *mee kiamoh*
My account number is...	Il mio numero di conto è... *eel meeo noomeroh dee kontoh eh*
My bank details are...	I miei dettagli bancari sono... *ee myayee dettalyee bankaree sonoh*

il passaporto
eel passaportoh
passport

il denaro
eel denaroh
money

il tasso di cambio
eel tassoh dee kambyo
exchange rate

Do I have...	Devo... *devoh*
...to key in my PIN?	...digitare il PIN? *deejeetareh eel peen*
...to sign here?	...firmare qui? *feermareh kwee*
The cash machine has swallowed my card	Lo sportello bancomat ha preso la mia carta *loh sportelloh bankomat ah presoh lah meea kartah*
Can I cash a check?	Posso incassare un assegno? *possoh eenkassareh oon assenyo*
Has my money arrived yet?	È arrivato il mio denaro? *eh arreevatoh eel meeo denaroh*
When does the bank open/close?	Quando apre/chiude la banca? *kwandoh apreh/kewdeh lah bankah*

lo sportello
bancomat
*loh sportelloh
bankomat*
cash machine

la carta di credito
*lah kartah dee
kredeetoh*
credit card

il libretto
degli assegni
*eel leebrettoh
delyee assenyee*
checkbook

STORES

la pescheria
lah peskerya
fish seller

il fruttivendolo
eel frooteevendoloh
produce stand

la drogheria
lah drogerya
grocery

la gastronomia
lah gastronomya
delicatessen

la panetteria
lah panetterya
bakery

la libreria
lah leebrerya
bookstore

il supermercato
eel soopermerkatoh
supermarket

la macelleria
lah machelerya
butcher

il tabaccaio
eel tabakkayo
tobacconist

il negozio di mobili
eel negotsyo dee mobeelee
furniture store

il negozio di calzature
eel negotsyo dee kaltsatooreh
shoe store

la boutique
lah booteek
boutique

la sartoria
lah sartorya
tailor

la gioielleria
lah joyellerya
jewelry store

la ferramenta
lah ferramentah
hardware store

AT THE MARKET

I would like...	Desidero... *deseederoh*
How much is this?	Quanto costa? *kwantoh kostah*
What's the price per kilo?	Quanto costa al chilo? *kwantoh kostah al keeloh*
It's too expensive	È troppo caro *eh troppoh karoh*
Do you have anything cheaper?	Avete qualcosa di meno caro? *aveteh kwalkosah dee menoh karoh*
That's fine, I'll take it	Va bene, lo prendo *vah beneh loh prendoh*
I'll take two kilos	Me ne dia due chili *meh neh dya dooeh keelee*
A kilo of...	Un chilo di... *oon keeloh dee*
Half a kilo of...	Mezzo chilo di... *medzo keeloh dee*
A little more, please	Un po' di più, per favore *oon poh dee pew pehr favoreh*
May I taste it?	Posso assaggiarlo/a? *possoh assadjarloh/ah*
That will be all, thank you	È tutto, la ringrazio *eh tootoh lah reengratsyo*

YOU MAY HEAR...

Posso aiutarla?
possoh ayewtarlah
May I help you?

Quanto ne vuole?
kwantoh neh vwoleh
How much would you like?

IN THE SUPERMARKET

Where is/are...

Dov'è/dove sono...
doveh/doveh sonoh

...the frozen foods

...i surgelati?
ee soorjelatee

...the beverage aisle?

...la corsia delle bibite?
lah korsya delleh beebeeteh

...the checkout?

...la cassa?
lah kassah

I'm looking for...

Sto cercando...
stoh cherkandoh

il carrello
eel karrelloh
grocery cart

il cestino
eel chesteenoh
basket

Do you have any more?

Ne avete ancora?
neh aveteh ankorah

Is this reduced?

È scontato?
eh skontatoh

Where do I pay?

Dove posso pagare?
doveh possoh pagareh

Shall I key in my PIN?

Devo digitare il PIN?
devoh deejeetareh eel peen

May I have a bag?

Posso avere un sacchetto?
possoh avereh oon sakettoh

FRUIT

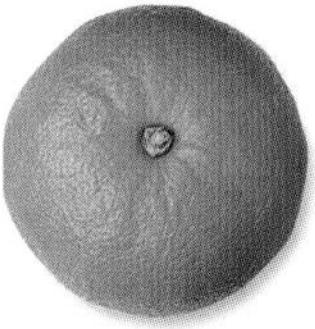

l'arancia
laranchya
orange

il limone
eel leemoneh
lemon

la pesca
lah peskah
peach

la pescanoce
lah peskanocheh
nectarine

il limone verde
*eel leemoneh
verdeh*
lime

la ciliegia
lah cheelyeja
cherries

l'albicocca
lalbeekokkah
apricot

la prugna
lah proonya
plum

il pompelmo
eel pompelmoh
grapefruit

il mirtillo
eel meerteeloh
blueberry

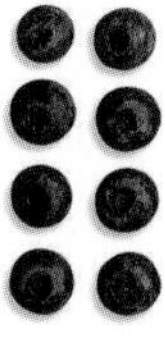

la fragola
la fragolah
strawberry

il lampone
eel lamponeh
raspberry

il melone
eel meloneh
melon

l'uva
loovah
grapes

la banana
lah bananah
banana

la melagrana
lah melagranah
pomegranate

la mela
lah melah
apple

la pera
lah perah
pear

l'ananas
lananas
pineapple

il mango
eel mangoh
mango

VEGETABLES

la patata
lah patatah
potato

la carota
lah karotah
carrot

il peperone
eel peperoneh
pepper

il peperoncino
*eel
peperoncheenoh*
chili pepper

la melanzana
lah melandzanah
eggplant

il pomodoro
eel pomodoroh
tomato

la cipolla
lah cheepolah
onion

l'aglio
lalyo
garlic

la cipollina
lah cheepoleenah
scallion

il porro
eel porroh
leek

il fungo
eel foongoh
mushroom

la zucchina
lah dzookeenah
zucchini

i piselli
ee peesellee
**garden
peas**

i fagiolini
ee fajoleenee
**green
beans**

il cetriolo
eel chetryoloh
cucumber

il sedano
eel sedanoh
celery

gli spinaci
lyee speenachee
spinach

il broccolo
eel brokkoloh
broccoli

la lattuga
lah latoogah
lettuce

il cavolo
eel kavoloh
cabbage

MEAT AND POULTRY

May I have...

Posso avere...
possoh avereh

...a slice of...?

...una fetta di...?
oonah fettah dee

...a piece of...?

...un pezzo di...?
oon pedzo dee

il prosciutto cotto
eel proshewtoh kottoh
cooked ham

la carne
tritata
*lah karneh
treetatah*
ground beef

la bistecca
lah beestekka
steak

il filetto
eel feelettoh
fillet

il prosciutto crudo
eel proshewtoh kroodoh
cured ham

il rognone
*eel
ronyoneh*
kidney

il pollo
eel polloh
chicken

il salame di
cinghiale
*eel salameh dee
cheengyaleh*
**wild boar
salami**

FISH AND SHELLFISH

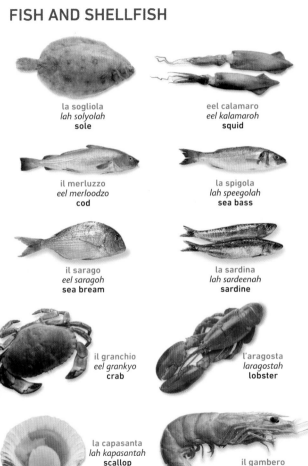

la sogliola
lah solyolah
sole

eel calamaro
eel kalamaroh
squid

il merluzzo
eel merloodzo
cod

la spigola
lah speegolah
sea bass

il sarago
eel saragoh
sea bream

la sardina
lah sardeenah
sardine

il granchio
eel grankyo
crab

l'aragosta
laragostah
lobster

la capasanta
lah kapasantah
scallop

il gambero
eel gamberoh
shrimp

BREAD AND CAKES

il pane casalingo
eel paneh kasaleengoh
home-baked bread

il pan marino
eel pan mareenoh
rosemary bread

i grissini
ee greeseenee
breadsticks

il panino
eel paneenoh
roll

il cornetto
eel kornettoh
croissant

la focaccia
lah fokatchya
foccaccia

il panettone
eel panettoneh
panettone

il panforte
eel panforteh
panforte

la crostata
al limone
*lah krostatah
al leemoneh*
lemon tart

la torta al
cioccolato
*lah tortah al
chokolatoh*
chocolate cake

DAIRY PRODUCE

il latte intero
eel lateh eenteroh
whole milk

parzialmente scremato
partsyalmenteh skrematoh
reduced-fat milk

lo yoghurt
loh yogoort
yogurt

il burro
eel booroh
butter

la panna
lah pannah
cream

la ricotta
lah reekottah
ricotta

il parmigiano
eel parmeejanoh
Parmesan cheese

la mozzarella
lah modzarellah
mozzarella

il provolone
eel provoloneh
Provolone

il pecorino
eel pekoreenoh
Pecorino

NEWSPAPERS AND MAGAZINES 🎧

Do you have...	Avete... *aveteh*
...a book of stamps?	...un carnet di francobolli? *oon karneh dee frankobollee*
...airmail stamps?	...francobolli di posta aerea? *frankobollee dee postah ahehrehah*
...a pack of envelopes?	...una confezione di buste? *oonah konfetsyoneh dee boosteh*
...some adhesive tape?	... del nastro adesivo? *del nastroh adeseevoh*

la cartolina
lah kartoleenah
postcard

la matita
lah mateetah
pencil

i francobolli
ee frankobolee
stamps

la penna
lah pennah
pen

YOU MAY HEAR...

Quale desidera?
kwaleh deseederah
**Which would
you like?**

Mi può dire la sua età?
*mee pwo deereh lah
sooa etah*
How old are you?

Ha la carta d'identità?
ah lah kartah deedenteetah
Do you have ID?

I'd like...

Vorrei...
vorray

...a pack of cigarettes

...un pacchetto di sigarette
oon pakkettoh dee seegaretteh

...a box of matches

...una scatola di cerini
oonah skatolah dee chereenee

i fumetti
ee foomettee
comic book

l'accendino
latchendeenoh
lighter

le matite colorate
leh mateeteh kolorateh
colored pencils

le gomme da masticare
leh gommeh dah masteekareh
chewing gum

le caramelle
leh karamelleh
candy

del tabacco
del tabakkoh
tobacco

la rivista
lah reeveestah
magazine

il quotidiano
eel kwoteedyanoh
newspaper

BUYING CLOTHES AND SHOES

I am looking for...	Sto cercando... *stoh cherkandoh*
I am size...	Porto la taglia... *portoh lah talya*
Do you have this...	Avete questo/a... *aveteh kwestoh/ah*
...in my size?	...nella mia taglia? *nellah meeah talya*
...in small?	...in taglia piccola? *een talya peekolah*
...in medium?	...in taglia media? *een talya medya*
...in large?	...in taglia grande? *een talya grandeh*
...in other colors?	...in altri colori? *een altree koloree*
May I try this on?	Posso provarlo/a? *possoh provarloh/ah*
It's...	È... *eh*
...too big	...troppo grande *troppoh grandeh*
...too small	...troppo piccolo/a *troppoh peekoloh/ah*
I need...	Ho bisogno di... *oh beezonyo dee*
...a larger size	...una taglia più grande *oonah talya pew grandeh*
...a smaller size	...una taglia più piccola *oonah talya pew peekolah*
I'll take this one, please	Prendo questo/a, grazie *prendoh kwestoh/ah gratsye*

| I take shoe size... | Mi serve un... |
| | *mee serveh oon* |

| Can I try... | Posso provare... |
| | *possoh provareh* |

| ...this pair? | ...questo paio? |
| | *kwestoh payo* |

| ...those in the window? | ...quelle in vetrina? |
| | *kwelleh een vetreenah* |

| These are... | Queste sono... |
| | *kwesteh sonoh* |

| ...too tight | ...troppo strette |
| | *troppoh stretteh* |

| ...too big | ...troppo larghe |
| | *troppoh largeh* |

| ...too small | ...troppo piccole |
| | *troppoh peekoleh* |

| ...uncomfortable | ...scomode |
| | *skomodeh* |

| Is there a bigger/ smaller size? | Avete un numero più grande/piccolo? |
| | *aveteh oon noomeroh pew grandeh/ peekoloh* |

CLOTHES AND SHOE SIZES GUIDE

Women's clothes sizes									
US	4	6	8	10	12	14	16	18	
Europe	34	36	38	40	42	44	46	48	

Men's clothes sizes									
US	36	38	40	42	44	46	48	50	
Europe	46	48	50	52	54	56	58	60	

Shoe sizes									
US	5	6	7	8	9	10	11	12	13
Europe	36	37	38	39	40	42	43	45	46

CLOTHES AND SHOES

il vestito
eel vesteetoh
dress

l'abito da sera
labeetoh dah serah
evening dress

la giacca
lah jakkah
jacket

il maglione
eel malyoneh
sweater

i jeans
ee jeens
jeans

la gonna
lah gonnah
skirt

la scarpa da
ginnastica
*lah skarpah dah
jeennasteekah*
sneakers

lo stivale
loh steevaleh
boots

la borsa
lah borzah
handbag

la cintura
lah cheentoorah
belt

il vestito da
uomo
*eel vesteetoh
dah womoh*
suit

il cappotto
eel kapottoh
coat

la camicia
lah kameechya
shirt

la t-shirt
lah t-shirt
T-shirt

i calzoncini
*ee
kaltsoncheenee*
shorts

il sandalo
eel sandaloh
sandal

la scarpa
con lacci
*lah skarpah
kon latchee*
tie shoe

la scarpa col
tacco alto
*lah skarpah kol
takko altoh*
**high-heeled
shoe**

l'infradito
leenfradeetoh
flip-flop

i calzini
ee kalseenee
socks

AT THE GIFT SHOP

I'd like to buy a gift for...	Vorrei acquistare un regalo per... *vorray akweestareh oon regaloh pehr*
...my mother/father	...mia madre/mio padre *meeah madreh/meeoh padreh*
...my daughter/son	...mia figlia/mio figlio *meeah feelya/meeoh feelyo*
...a child	...un/a bambino/a *oon/ah bambeenoh/ah*
...a friend	...un/a amico/a *oon/ah ameekoh/ah*
Can you recommend something?	Mi può consigliare qualcosa? *mee pwo konseelyareh kwalkosah*
Do you have a box for it?	Ha la scatola? *ah lah skatolah*
Can you gift-wrap it?	Può fare un pacchetto regalo? *pwo fareh oon pakettoh regaloh*

il bracciale
eel bratchyaleh
bracelet

i gemelli
ee jemellee
cufflinks

la collana
lah kollanah
necklace

l'orologio
lorolojoh
watch

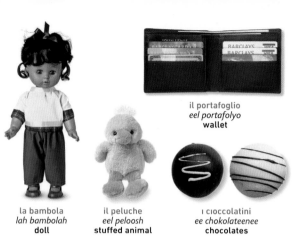

la bambola	il peluche	i cioccolatini
lah bambolah	*eel peloosh*	*ee chokolateenee*
doll	**stuffed animal**	**chocolates**

il portafoglio
eel portafolyo
wallet

I want a souvenir of...	Desidero un souvenir di...
	deseederoh oon soovenir dee
Have you anything cheaper?	Ha qualcosa di meno caro?
	ah kwalkosah dee menoh karoh
Is there a guarantee?	È coperto/a da garanzia?
	eh kopertoh/ah dah garantsya

YOU MAY HEAR...

È un regalo?
eh oon regaloh
Is it a present?

Vuole un pacchetto regalo?
woleh oon pakettoh regaloh
Shall I gift-wrap it?

PHOTOGRAPHY

I'd like this film developed	Vorrei sviluppare questa pellicola *vorray sveeloopareh kwestah* *pelleekolah*
Do you have an express service?	Avete un servizio espresso? *aveteh oon serveetsyo espressoh*
Does it cost more?	Costa di più? *kostah dee pew*
I'd like...	Vorrei... *vorray*
...the one-hour service	...lo sviluppo in un'ora *loh sveeloopoh een oonorah*

la fotocamera
digitale
lah fotokamerah
deejeetaleh
digital camera

la scheda di memoria
lah skedah dee
memorya
memory card

la cornice
lah korneeche
photo frame

l'album delle fotografie
lalboom delleh fotografye
photo album

...a battery

...una batteria
oonah battereeya

**Can you print from
this memory stick?**

Potete stampare da questa
chiavetta USB?
*poteteh stampareh dah kwestah
kyakettah oo-es-bee*

gli obiettivi
lyee obyeteevee
lens

la fotocamera
lah fotokamerah
camera

la borsa per
fotocamera
*lah borsah pehr
fotokamerah*
camera bag

il flash
eel flash
flash gun

YOU MAY HEAR...

Quale formato di foto
desidera?
*kwaleh formatoh
deseedeerah*
**What size prints do
you want?**

Opache o lucide?
opakeh oh loocheedeh?
Matte or gloss?

AT THE POST OFFICE 🎧

I'd like...
Vorrei...
vorray

...three stamps, please
...tre francobolli, per favore
treh frankobollee pehr favoreh

...to register this letter
...inviare una raccomandata
eenvyareh oonah rakomandatah

...to send this airmail
...inviare questo per posta aerea
eenvyareh kwestoh pehr postah ahehreha

i francobolli
ee frankobollee
stamps

la busta
lah boostah
envelope

la posta aerea
lah postah ahehreha
airmail

la cartolina
lah kartoleenah
postcard

YOU MAY HEAR...

Cosa contiene?
kozah kontyeneh
What are the contents?

Qual è il suo valore?
kwaleh eel soo-oh valoreh
What is their value?

Riempia questo modulo
ryempya kwestoh modooloh
Fill out this form

How much is...?	Quanto costa... *kwantoh kostah*
...a letter to...	...una lettera per... *oonah letterah pehr*
...a postcard to...	...una cartolina per... *oonah kartoleenah pehr*
...the United States	...gli Stati Uniti *lyee statee ooneetee*
...Great Britain	...la Gran Bretagna *lah gran bretanya*
...Canada	...il Canada *eel kanadah*
...Australia	...l'Australia *lowstralya*
May I have a receipt?	Posso avere la ricevuta? *possoh avereh lah reechevootah*
Where can I mail this?	Dove posso imbucare questa lettera? *doveh possoh eembookareh kwestah letterah*

il pacco
eel pakoh
package

il corriere
eel korryereh
courier

la cassetta delle lettere
lah kassettah delleh lettereh
mailbox

il postino
eel posteenoh
letter carrier

TELEPHONES

Where is the nearest phone shop?	Dove è il negozio di telefoni più vicino? *Doveh eel negotsyo dee telehfonee pew veecheenoh*
Who's speaking?	Pronto, chi parla? *prontoh kee parlah*
Hello, this is...	Pronto, sono... *prontoh sonoh*
I'd like to speak to...	Vorrei parlare con... *vorray parlareh kon*

il telefono
eel telefonoh
phone

lo smatphone
loh smartphone
smartphone

il cellulare
eel chelloolareh
cell phone

la segreteria telefonica
lah segreterya telefoneekah
answering machine

il telefono a
moneta
*eel telefonoh
ah monetah*
**coin-operated
phone**

INTERNET

Is there an internet café near here?
C'è un Internet cafè qui vicino?
che oon eenternet kafeh kwee veecheenoh

How much do you charge?
Quanto costa?
kwantoh kostah

Do you have wireless internet?
Avete un sistema Internet wireless?
aveteh oon seestemah eenternet wireless

Can I check my emails?
Posso controllare le mie e-mail?
possoh kontrollareh leh meeyeh emayl

I need to send an email
Devo inviare un'e-mail
devoh eenvyareh oonemayl

What's your email address?
Qual è il suo indirizzo e-mail?
kwaleh eel soo-oh eendeereedzo emayl

My email address is...
Il mio indirizzo e-mail è...
eel meeoh eendeereedzo emayl eh

il computer portatile
eel compewter portateeleh
laptop

la tastiera
lah tastyerah
keyboard

il sito Web
eel seetoh web
website

l'e-mail
lemayl
email

SIGHTSEEING

Most Italian cities and towns have a tourist information office, which is usually situated near the train station or town hall. The staff will advise you on local places of interest to visit and cultural events. In Italy, most national museums close on Mondays as well as on public holidays, so make sure that you check the opening times before visiting.

AT THE TOURIST OFFICE

Where is the tourist information office?
Dov'è l'ufficio del turismo?
doveh loofeechyo del tooreesmoh

Can you recommend...
Può consigliarmi...
pwo konseelyarmee

...a guided tour?
...una visita guidata?
oonah veeseetah gweedatah

...an excursion?
...una gita?
oonah jeetah

Is there a museum or art gallery?
C'è un museo o una galleria d'arte?
che oon moozeoh oh oonah gallereeya darteh

Is it open to the public?
È aperto/a al pubblico?
eh apertoh/ah al poobleekoh

Is there wheelchair access?
C'è un accesso per disabili?
che oon atchessoh pehr deezabeelee

Does it close...
È chiuso/a...
eh kewsoh/ah

...on Sundays?
...la domenica?
lah domeneekah

...on public holidays?
...nei giorni festivi?
nay jornee festeevee

How long does it take to get there?
Quanto ci vuole per arrivarci?
kwantoh chee vwoleh pehr areevarchee

Do you have...
Avete...
aveteh

...a street map?
...una cartina?
oonah karteenah

...a guide?
...una guida?
oonah gweedah

...any leaflets?
...degli opuscoli?
dehlyee opooskolee

VISITING PLACES

What time...	A che ora... *ah ke orah*
...do you open?	...apre? *apreh*
...do you close?	...chiude? *kewdeh*
I'd like two entrance tickets	Vorrei due biglietti d'entrata *vorray dooeh beelyettee dentratah*
Two adults, please	Due adulti, per favore *dooeh adooltee pehr favoreh*
A family ticket	Un biglietto famiglia *oon beelyettoh fameelya*
How much does it cost?	Quanto costa? *kwantoh kostah*
Are there reductions for...	Ci sono delle riduzioni per... *chee sonoh delleh reedootsyonee pehr*
...children?	...i bambini? *ee bambeenee*
...students?	...gli studenti? *lyee stoodentee*

la pianta della città
lah pyantah dellah cheetah
street map

il biglietto d'entrata
eel beelyettoh dentratah
entrance ticket

l'ufficio del turismo
loofeechyo del tooreesmoh
tourist office

l'accesso disabili
latchessoh deezabeelee
wheelchair access

Can I buy a guidebook?	Posso acquistare una guida? *possoh akweestareh oonah gweedah*
Is there...	C'è... *che*
...an audio guide?	...un'audio guida? *oonowdyo gweedah*
...a guided tour?	...una visita guidata? *oonah veeseetah gweedatah*
...an elevator?	...un ascensore? *oon ashenzoreh*
...a bus tour?	...un giro turistico in autobus? *oon jeeroh tooreesteeko een owtoboos*
When is the next tour?	Quando parte il prossimo giro turistico? *kwandoh parteh eel proseemoh jeeroh tooreesteeko*

il tour in autobus
eel tour een owtoboos
tour bus

YOU MAY HEAR...

Quanti anni ha?
kwantee annee ah
How old are you?

Possiede una carta studenti?
possyedeh oonah kartah stoodentee
Do you have a student ID?

FINDING YOUR WAY

Excuse me	Mi scusi *mee skoozee*
Can you help me?	Mi può aiutare? *mee pwo ayewtareh*
Is this the way to...?	È questa la strada per...? *eh kwestah lah stradah pehr*
How do I get to...?	Come raggiungo...? *komeh radjewngoh*
...the town center?	...il centro della città? *eel chentroh dellah cheetah*
...the station?	...la stazione? *lah statsyoneh*
...the museum?	...il museo? *eel moozeoh*
...the art gallery?	...la galleria d'arte? *lah gallereeya darteh*
How long does it take?	Quanto tempo s'impiega? *kwantoh tempoh seempyegah*
Is it far?	È lontano? *eh lontanoh*
Can you show me on the map?	Me lo può indicare sulla cartina? *meh loh pwo eendeekareh soolah karteenah*

YOU MAY HEAR...

Non è lontano
non eh lontanoh
It's not far away

Ci vogliono dieci minuti
chee volyonoh deeaychee meenootee
It takes ten minutes.

YOU MAY HEAR...

Siamo qui
syamoh kwee
We are here

Vada sempre dritto...
vadah sempreh dreetoh
Keep going straight...

...fino alla fine della via
feenoh allah feeneh dellah veeya
...to the end of the street

...fino al semaforo
feenoh al semaforoh
...to the traffic lights

...fino alla piazza principale
feenoh allah pyadza preencheepaleh
...to the main square

Di qua
dee kwa
This way

Di là
dee lah
That way

Svolti a destra al/alla...
svoltee ah destrah al/allah
Turn right at...

Svolti a sinistra al/alla...
svoltee ah seeneestrah al/allah
Turn left at...

Prenda la prima...
prendah lah preemah
Take the first...

...a sinistra/a destra
ah seeneestrah/ah destrah
...on the left/right

È davanti a lei
eh davantee ah lay
It's in front of you

È dietro di lei
eh deeyehtroh dee lay
It's behind you

È di fronte a lei
eh dee fronteh ah lay
It's opposite you

È vicino a...
eh veecheenoh ah
It's next to...

C'è un'indicazione
che ooneendeekatsyoneh
It's signed

È là
eh lah
It's over there

PLACES TO VISIT

il municipio
eel mooneecheepyo
town hall

il ponte
eel ponteh
bridge

il museo
eel moozeoh
museum

la galleria d'arte
lah gallereeya darteh
art gallery

il monumento
eel monoomentoh
monument

la chiesa
lah kyezah
church

il paese
eel paheseh
village

la cattedrale
lah katedraleh
cathedral

il castello
eel kastelloh
castle

il faro
eel faroh
lighthouse

il porto
eel portoh
harbor

il vigneto
eel veenyetoh
vineyard

il parco
eel parkoh
park

la costa
lah kostah
coast

la cascata
lah kaskatah
waterfall

le montagne
leh montanye
mountains

OUTDOOR ACTIVITIES

Where can we go... | Dove possiamo...
doveh possyamoh

...horseback riding? | ...andare a cavallo?
andareh ah kavalloh

...fishing? | ...andare a pescare?
andareh ah peskareh

...swimming? | ...nuotare?
nwotareh

...walking? | ...fare un'escursione a piedi?
fareh oon eskoorzyoneh ah pyedee

Can we... | Possiamo...
possyamoh

...rent equipment? | ...noleggiare l'attrezzatura?
noledjareh lattredzatoorah

...take lessons? | ...prendere delle lezioni?
prendereh delleh letsyonee

How much per hour? | Quanto costa all'ora?
kwantoh kostah allorah

I'm a beginner | Sono un/a principiante
sonoh oon/ah preencheepyanteh

I'm very experienced | Ho una buona esperienza
Oh oonah bwonah esperyentsah

Where's the amusement park? | Dov'è il parco dei divertimenti?
doveh eel parkoh day deeverteementee

Can the children go on all the rides? | I bambini possono andare su tutte le giostre?
ee bambeenee possonoh andareh soo tooteh leh jostreh

Is there a playground? | C'è un'area giochi?
che oon ahrehah jokee

Is it safe for children? | È sicura per i bambini?
eh seekoorah pehr ee bambeenee

lo zoo
loh dzoh
zoo

l'area giochi
larehah jokee
playground

il picnic
eel picnic
picnic

il luna park
eel loonah park
fairground

pescare
peskareh
fishing

andare a cavallo
andareh ah kavalloh
horseback riding

il parco safari
eel parkoh safaree
safari park

il parco a tema
eel parkoh ah temah
amusement park

SPORTS AND LEISURE

Italy can offer the traveler a wide range of cultural events, entertainments, leisure activities, and sports. The Italians are proud of their rich artistic and musical heritage, and their distinctive culture is very important to them. For the sports enthusiast, a wide range of spectator sports and facilities are available, from winter sports, climbing, and hiking in the Alps and Appenines to watersports around the coast and on inland lakes. Soccer is the national game and you can watch a *Serie* A match.

LEISURE TIME

I like...	Mi piace/piacciono... *mee pyaceh/pyatchyonoh*
...art and painting	...l'arte e la pittura *larteh eh lah peetoorah*
...movies and film	...i film e il cinema *ee film eh eel cheenemah*
...the theater	...il teatro *eel tehatroh*
...opera	...l'opera *loperah*
I prefer...	Preferisco... *prefereeskoh*
...reading books	...leggere libri *ledjereh leebree*
...listening to music	...ascoltare musica *askoltareh moozeekah*
...watching sports	...guardare lo sport *gwardareh loh sport*
...going to concerts	...andare ai concerti *andareh ahee konchertee*
...dancing	...ballare *ballareh*
...going to clubs	...andare in discoteca *andareh een deeskotekah*
...going out with friends	...uscire con gli amici *oosheereh kon lyee ameechee*
I don't like...	Non mi piace... *non mee pyacheh*
That doesn't interest me	Non mi interessa *non mee eenteressah*

AT THE BEACH

Can I rent...	Posso noleggiare... *possoh noledjareh*
...a jet ski?	...una moto d'acqua? *oonah motoh dakwa*
...a beach umbrella?	...un ombrellone da mare? *oon ombrelloneh dah mareh*
...a surfboard?	...una tavola da surf? *oonah tavolah dah surf*
...a wetsuit?	...una muta subacquea? *oonah mootah soobakweah*

il telo da mare
eel teloh dah mareh
beach towel

la sedia a sdraio
lah sedya ah sdrayo
deck chair

il pallone da spiaggia
eel palloneh dah speeadjah
beach ball

il lettino sdraio
eel leteenoh sdrayo
lounge chair

YOU MAY HEAR...

Divieto di balneazione
deevyetoh dee balneatsyoneh
No swimming

Spiaggia chiusa
speeadja kewsah
Beach closed

How much does it cost?	Quanto costa? *kwantoh kostah*
Can I go water-skiing?	Posso fare dello sci d'acqua? *possoh fareh delloh shee dakwa*
Is there a lifeguard?	C'è il bagnino? *che eel baneenoh*
Is it safe to...	È sicuro... *eh seekooroh*
...swim here?	...nuotare qui? *nwotareh kwee*
...surf here?	...fare del surf qui? *fareh del surf kwee*

gli occhiali da sole
lyee okeealee dah soleh
sunglasses

il cappello da sole
eel kappeloh dah soleh
sunhat

le pinne
leh peenneh
fins

la lozione solare
lah lotsyoneh solareh
suntan lotion

il bikini
eel beekeenee
bikini

la maschera e il boccaglio
lah maskerah eh eel bokalyo
mask and snorkel

AT THE SWIMMING POOL 🎧

What time...	Quando... *kwandoh*
...does the pool open?	...apre la piscina? *apreh lah peesheenah*
...does the pool close?	...chiude la piscina? *kewdeh lah peesheenah*
Is it...	È... *eh*
...an indoor pool?	...una piscina coperta? *oonah peesheenah kopertah*
...an outdoor pool?	...una piscina all'aperto? *oonah peesheenah alapertoh*
Is there a children's pool?	C'è una piscina per bambini? *che oonah peesheenah pehr bambeenee*
Where are the changing rooms?	Dove sono gli spogliatoi? *doveh sonoh lyee spolyatoy*
Is it safe to dive?	È sicuro tuffarsi? *eh seekooroh toofarsee*

i braccioli
ee bratchyolee
water wings

la tavoletta
lah tavolettah
float

il costume
eel kostoomeh
swimsuit

gli occhialini
lyee okyaleenee
swimming goggles

AT THE GYM

l'ellittica
lelleeteekah
cross trainer

la bicicletta
lah beecheeklettah
exercise bike

il vogatore
eel vogatoreh
rowing machine

la step machine
lah step machine
step machine

Is there a gym?	C'è una palestra? *che oonah palestrah*
Is it free for guests?	È gratuita per i clienti? *eh gratooeetah pehr ee klyentee*
Do I have to wear sneakers?	Devo indossare le scarpe da ginnastica? *devoh eendossareh leh skarpeh dah jeennasteekah*
Do I need an introductory session?	Devo fare una sessione introduttiva? *devoh fareh oonah sessyoneh introdootteevah*
Do you hold...	Offrite... *offreeteh*
...aerobics classes?	...lezioni di aerobica? *letsyonee dee aerobeekah*
...Pilates classes?	...lezioni di Pilates? *letsyonee dee pilates*
...yoga classes?	...lezioni di yoga? *letsyonee dee yogah*

BOATING AND SAILING

Can I rent...	Posso noleggiare... *possoh noledjareh*
...a dinghy?	...un gommone? *oon gommoneh*
...a windsurf board?	...una tavola da windsurf? *oonah tavolah dah windsurf*
...a canoe?	...una canoa? *oonah kanoah*
Do you offer sailing lessons?	Offrite lezioni di vela? *offreeteh letsyonee dee velah*
Do you have a mooring?	Avete un ormeggio? *aveteh oon ormedjoh*
How much is it for the night?	Quanto costa per notte? *kwantoh kostah pehr notteh*
Where can I buy gas?	Dove posso acquistare del gasolio? *doveh possoh akweestareh del gazolyo*
Where is the marina?	Dov'è il porticciolo? *doveh eel porteetchyoloh*
My...is broken	Il mio/la mia...non funziona *eel meeoh/lah meeah...non foontsyonah*
Can you repair it?	Potete ripararlo/a? *poteteh reepararloh/ah*
Are there life jackets?	Ci sono dei giubbotti di salvataggio? *chee sonoh day jewbottee dee salvatadjoh*

il giubbotto di
salvataggio
*eel jewbottoh
dee salvatadjoh*
life jacket

la bussola
lah boosolah
compass

WINTER SPORTS

I would like to rent...	Desidero noleggiare... *deseederoh noledjareh*
...some skis	...un paio di sci *oon payo dee shee*
...some ski boots	...un paio di scarponi *oon payo dee skarponee*
...some poles	...un paio di racchette *oon payo dee raketteh*
...a snowboard	...uno snowboard *oonoh snowboard*
...a helmet	...un casco *oon kaskoh*
When does...	Quando... *kwandoh*
...the chair lift start?	...apre la seggiovia? *apreh lah sedjoveeya*
...the cable car finish?	...chiude la funivia? *kewdeh lah fooneeveeya*
How much is a lift pass?	Quanto costa un pass? *kwantoh kostah oon pass*
Can I take skiing lessons?	Posso prendere delle lezioni di sci? *possoh prendereh delleh letsyonee dee shee*

YOU MAY HEAR...

È un principiante?
eh oon preencheepeeanteh
Are you a beginner?

Deve lasciare un deposito
deveh lashyareh oon deposeetoh
I need a deposit

BALL GAMES

I like playing...	Mi piace giocare a... *mee pyacheh jokareh ah*
...soccer	...pallone *palloneh*
...tennis	...tennis *tennis*
...golf	...golf *golf*
...badminton	...volano *volahnoh*
...squash	...squash *skwosh*
...baseball	...baseball *besboll*
Where is the nearest...	Dov'è il più vicino... *doveh eel pew veecheenoh*
...tennis court?	...campo da tennis? *kampoh dah tennis*
...golf course?	...campo da golf? *kampoh dah golf*
...sports center?	...centro sportivo? *chentroh sporteevoh*

il pallone
eel palloneh
soccer ball

il canestro
eel kanestroh
basket

il guanto da baseball
eel gwantoh dah besball
baseball glove

May I book a court...	Posso prenotare un campo... *possoh prenotareh oon kampoh*
...for two hours?	...per due ore? *pehr dooeh oreh*
...at three o'clock?	...per le tre? *pehr leh tray*
What shoes are allowed?	Quali scarpe sono permesse? *kwalee skarpeh sonoh permesseh*
Can I rent...	Posso noleggiare... *possoh noledjareh*
...a tennis racket?	...una racchetta da tennis? *oonah rakettah dah tennis*
...some balls?	...delle palle? *delleh palleh*
...a set of clubs?	...un set di mazze? *oon set dee madze*
...a golf buggy?	...il carrello elettrico? *eel karreloh elettreekoh*

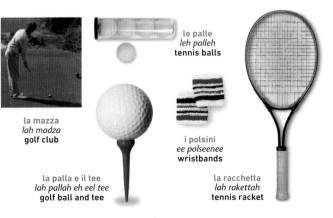

le palle
leh palleh
tennis balls

la mazza
lah madza
golf club

i polsini
ee polseenee
wristbands

la palla e il tee
lah pallah eh eel tee
golf ball and tee

la racchetta
lah rakettah
tennis racket

GOING OUT

Where is...	Dov'è... *doveh*
...the opera house?	...il teatro dell'opera? *eel teatroh delloperah*
...a jazz club?	...il jazz club? *eel jazz clab*
Do I have to book in advance?	Devo prenotare in anticipo? *devoh prenotareh een anteecheepoh*
I'd like...tickets	Vorrei...biglietti *vorray…beelyettee*
I'd like seats...	Vorrei dei posti... *vorray day postee*
...at the back	...in fondo *een fondoh*
...at the front	...davanti *davantee*
...in the middle	...nel mezzo *nel medzo*
...in the balcony	...in galleria *een gallereeya*
Can I buy a program?	Posso acquistare un programma? *possoh akweestareh oon programmah*
Is there live music?	C'è musica dal vivo? *che moozeekah dal veevoh*

YOU MAY HEAR...

Spenga il cellulare
spengah eel chelloolareh
**Turn off your
cell phone**

Torni a sedere
tornee ah sedereh
**Return to your
seats**

il musicista
eel moozeecheestah
musician

il teatro
eel teatroh
theater

il teatro dell'opera
eel teatroh delloperah
opera house

la discoteca
lah deeskotehkah
nightclub

il/la cantante
eel/lah kantanteh
singer

il pianista
eel pyaneestah
pianist

il cinema
eel cheenemah
movie theater

i popcorn
ee popcorn
popcorn

il casinò
eel kaseenoh
casino

la danza
lah dandza
ballet

GALLERIES AND MUSEUMS

What are the opening
hours?

Qual è l'orario di apertura?
kwaleh loraryo dapertoorah

Are there guided tours
in English?

Ci sono delle visite guidate in inglese?
*chee sonoh delleh veezeeteh
gweedateh een eenglezeh*

When does the tour
leave?

Quando inizia la visita?
kwandoh eeneetsya lah veezeetah

How much does it cost?

Quanto costa?
kwantoh kostah

How long does it take?

Quanto dura?
kwantoh doorah

Do you have an audio
guide?

Avete delle guide audio?
aveteh delleh gweedeh owdyo

Do you have a guidebook
in English?

Avete una guida in inglese?
aveteh oonah gweedah een eenglezeh

Can you direct me to...?

Mi può indirizzare a...?
mee pwo eendeereetsareh ah

Is (flash) photography
allowed?

Sono permesse le fotografie (con il
flash)?
*sonoh permesseh leh fotografye
(kon eel flash)*

la statua
lah statwa
statue

il busto
eel boostoh
bust

I'd really like to see...	Mi piacerebbe molto visitare... *mee pyacherebbeh moltoh veezeetareh*
Who painted this?	Chi è l'autore di questo quadro? *ki eh lowtoreh dee kwestoh kwadroh*
How old is it?	A quando risale? *ah kwandoh reesaleh*
Are there wheelchair ramps?	Ci sono delle rampe per disabili? *chee sonoh delleh rampeh pehr deezabeelee*
Is there an elevator?	C'è un ascensore? *che oon ashensoreh*
Where are the restrooms?	Dov'è la toilette? *doveh lah twalet*
I've lost my group	Ho perso il mio gruppo *oh persoh eel meeoh grooppoh*

il dipinto
eel deepeentoh
painting

il disegno
eel deesenyo
drawing

l'incisione
leencheesyoneh
engraving

il manoscritto
eel manoskreettoh
manuscript

HOME ENTERTAINMENT

How do I...	Come... *komeh*
...turn on the television?	...accendo il televisore? *atchendoh eel televeezoreh*
...change channels?	...cambio i canali? *kambyo ee kanalee*
...turn up the volume?	...alzo il volume? *altso eel voloomeh*
...turn down the volume?	...abbasso il volume? *abassoh eel voloomeh*
Do you have satellite TV?	Avete una TV satellitare? *aveteh oonah TV satelleetareh*
Where can I buy...	Dove posso acquistare... *doveh possoh akweestareh*
...a DVD?	...un DVD? *oon deeveedee*
...a music CD?	...un CD musicale? *oon cheedee moozeekaleh*
...an audio CD?	...un CD audio? *oon cheedee owdyo*

il lettore DVD
eel lettoreh deeveedee
DVD player

il televisore a schermo panoramico
eel televeezoreh ah skermoh panorameekoh
widescreen TV

il telecomando
eel telekomandoh
remote control

il videogioco
eel videojokoh
video game

l penna USB
lah pennah uh-es-bee
USB flash drive

il portatile
eel portateeleh
laptop

la radio
lah radyo
radio

l'hard drive
lard drive
hard drive

il mouse
eel mows
mouse

Can I use this to...	Posso usarlo per... *possoh oozarloh pehr*
...go online?	...accedere ad Internet? *atchedereh ad eenternet*
Is it broadband/wifi?	È a banda larga/wifi? *eh ah bandah largah/wifi*
How do I...	Come... *komeh*
...log on?	...mi conetto? *mee konnettoh*
...log out?	...mi disconetto? *mee deeskonnettoh*
...reboot?	...riavvio il computer? *reeyaveeyo eel compooter*

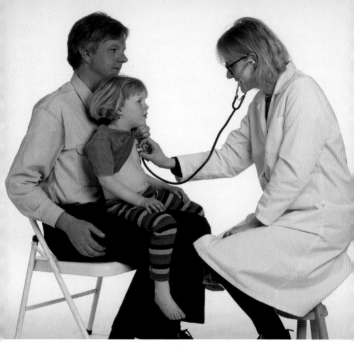

HEALTH

EU nationals receive free emergency medical care in Italy,
provided they produce a European Health Insurance Card.
Visitors from other countries should check that their health
insurance covers them for medical treatment abroad, or
purchase special travel insurance. It is a good idea to
familiarize yourself with a few basic phrases in case you
need to visit a pharmacy or doctor.

USEFUL PHRASES

I need a doctor	Ho bisogno di un medico *oh beezonyo dee oon medeekoh*
I would like an appointment...	Vorrei prendere un appuntamento... *vorray prendereh oon apoontamentoh*
...as soon as possible	...al più presto possibile *al pew prestoh posseebeeleh*
...today	...per oggi *pehr odjee*
...tomorrow	...per domani *pehr domanee*
It's very urgent	È molto urgente *eh moltoh oorjenteh*
I have a European Health Insurance Card	Possiedo una carta di assistenza sanitaria europea *possyedoh oonah kartah dee asseestentsa saneetarya ehooropayah*
I have health insurance	Ho un'assicurazione sanitaria *oh oon asseekooratsyoneh saneetarya*
May I have a receipt?	Posso avere la ricevuta? *possoh avereh lah reechevootah*
Where is the nearest...	Dov'è la più vicino/a... *doveh lah pew veecheenoh/ah*
...pharmacy?	...farmacia? *farmacheeya*
...doctor's office?	...ambulatorio medico? *amboolatoryo medeekoh*
...hospital?	...ospedale? *ospedaleh*
...dentist?	...dentista? *denteestah*

AT THE PHARMACY

What can I take for...?	Cosa posso prendere per...? *kozah possoh prendereh pehr*
How many should I take?	Quante ne devo prendere? *kwanteh neh devoh prendereh*
Is it safe for children?	È sicuro/a per i bambini? *eh seekooroh/ah pehr ee bambeenee*
Are there side effects?	Ha degli effetti indesiderati? *ah delyee effetee eendeseederatee*
Do you have that...	Questo prodotto viene venduto... *kwestoh prodottoh vyeneh vendootoh*
...as in tablet form?	...in compresse? *een kompresseh*
...in capsule form?	...in capsule? *een kapsooleh*
I'm allergic to...	Sono allergico/a a... *sonoh allerjeekoh/ah ah*
I'm already taking...	Sto già prendendo... *stoh jah prendendoh*
Do I need a prescription?	Ho bisogno della ricetta medica? *oh beezonyo dellah reechettah medeekah*

YOU MAY HEAR...

Prenda questo/a... volte al giorno
prendah kwestoh/ah...volteh al jornoh
Take this...times a day

Durante i pasti
dooranteh ee pastee
With food

le bende
leh bendeh
bandage

il cerotto
eel cherottoh
**adhesive
bandage**

le capsule
leh kapsooleh
capsules

le compresse
leh compresseh
pills

la pomata
lah pomatah
ointment

le supposte
leh soopposteh
suppositories

le gocce
leh goccheh
drops

l'inalatore
leenalatoreh
inhaler

lo spray
loh spry
spray

lo sciroppo
loh sheeroppoh
syrup

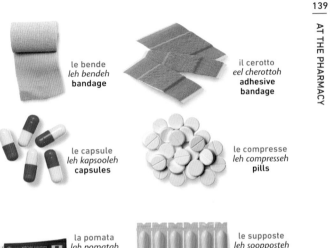

THE HUMAN BODY

I have hurt my...

Mi sono fatto/a male al/alla...
mee sonoh fattoh/ah maleh al/allah

il gomito
eel gomeetoh
elbow

il braccio
eel bratchyo
arm

la testa
lah testah
head

la spalla
lah spallah
shoulder

il collo
eel kolloh
neck

il torace
eel torache
chest

lo stomaco
loh stomakoh
stomach

la gamba
lah gambah
leg

il ginocchio
eel jeenokyo
knee

il piede
eel pyedeh
foot

FACE

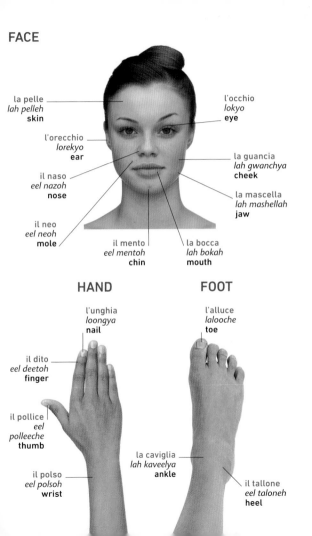

la pelle
lah pelleh
skin

l'occhio
lokyo
eye

l'orecchio
lorekyo
ear

la guancia
lah gwanchya
cheek

il naso
eel nazoh
nose

la mascella
lah mashellah
jaw

il neo
eel neoh
mole

il mento
eel mentoh
chin

la bocca
lah bokah
mouth

HAND

l'unghia
loongya
nail

il dito
eel deetoh
finger

il pollice
eel polleeche
thumb

il polso
eel polsoh
wrist

FOOT

l'alluce
lalooche
toe

la caviglia
lah kaveelya
ankle

il tallone
eel taloneh
heel

FEELING SICK

I don't feel well	Non mi sento bene *non mee sentoh beneh*
I feel sick	Mi sento male *mee sentoh maleh*
I have...	Ho... *Oh*
...an ear ache	...mal d'orecchio *mal dorekyo*
...a stomach ache	...mal di stomaco *mal dee stomakoh*
...a sore throat	...la gola infiammata *lah golah enfyammatah*
...a temperature	...la febbre *lah febbreh*
...hayfever	...il raffreddore da fieno *eel rafreddoreh dah fyenoh*
...constipation	...costipazione *kosteepatsyoneh*
...diarrhea	...diarrea *dyareah*
...toothache	...mal di denti *mal dee dentee*
I've been stung by...	Mi ha punto... *mee ah poontoh*
...a bee/wasp	...un'ape/una vespa *oonapeh/oonah vespah*
...a jellyfish	...una medusa *oonah medoosah*
I've been bitten by...	Mi ha morso... *mee ah morsoh*
...a dog	...un cane *oon kaneh*

INJURIES

il morso
eel morsoh
bite

la puntura
lah poontoorah
sting

la frattura
lah fratoorah
fracture

l'escoriazione
leskoryatsyoneh
graze

la scheggia
lah skedjah
splinter

la bruciatura
lah broochyatoorah
burn

il taglio
eel talyo
cut

l'ematoma
lematomah
bruise

la distorsione
lah deestorsyoneh
sprain

la scottatura solare
lah skotatoorah solareh
sunburn

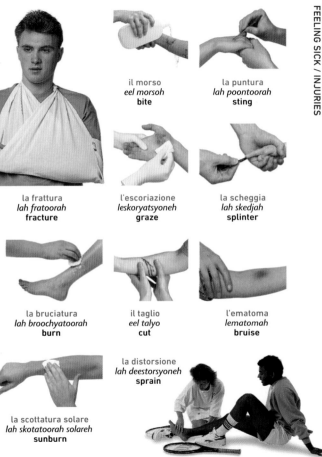

AT THE DOCTOR 🎧

I'm...	Sto... *stoh*
...vomiting	...vomitando *vomeetandoh*
...bleeding	...perdendo sangue *perdendoh sangwe*
...dizzy	...ho le vertigini *oh leh verteejeenee*
...feeling faint	...mi sento svenire *mee sentoh sveneereh*
...pregnant	...sono incinta *sonoh eencheentah*
...diabetic	...ho il diabete *oh eel dyabeteh*
...epileptic	...sono epilettico/a *sonoh epeeletteekoh/ah*
I have...	Soffro di... *soffroh dee*
...arthritis	...artrite *artreeteh*
...a heart condition	...una patologia cardiaca *oonah patolojeea kardeeakah*
...high blood pressure	...elevata pressione sanguigna *elevatah pressyoneh sangweenya*

YOU MAY HEAR...

Cosa c'è che non va?
kozah che ke non vah
What's wrong?

Dove le fa male?
doveh leh fah maleh
Where does it hurt?

Posso visitarla?
possoh veezeetarlah
May I examine you?

ILLNESS

la tosse
lah tosseh
cough

l'asma
lasmah
asthma

il raffreddore
eel rafreddoreh
cold

l'influenza
leenflooentsa
the flu

lo starnuto
loh starnootoh
sneeze

i crampi
ee krampee
stomach cramps

la nausea
lah nowzeah
nausea

l'eruzione cutanea
lerootsyoneh kootaneah
rash

il sangue dal naso
eel sangwe dal nasoh
nosebleed

il mal di testa
eel mal dee testah
headache

AT THE HOSPITAL

Can you help me?	Mi può aiutare? *mee pwo ayewtareh*
I need...	Ho bisogno di... *oh beezonyo dee*
...a doctor	...un dottore *oon dottoreh*
...a nurse	...un'infermiera *oon eenfermyerah*
Where is...	Dov'è... *doveh*
...the emergency room?	...il Pronto Soccorso? *eel prontoh sokorsoh*
...the children's ward?	...il reparto pediatrico? *eel repartoh pedyatreeko*
...the X-ray department?	...il reparto di radiologia? *eel repartoh dee radyolojah*
...the elevator/stairs?	...l'ascensore/la scala? *lashensoreh/lah skalah*

l'iniezione
leenyetsyoneh
injection

la radiografia
lah radyografya
X-ray

le analisi
del sangue
*leh analeezee
del sangwe*
blood test

l'ecografia,
la TAC
*lekografya
lah tac*
CT scan

...the waiting room?

...la sala d'attesa?
lah salah dattezah

...the intensive care unit?

...il reparto di terapia intensiva?
eel repartoh dee terapya eentenseevah

I think I've broken...

Penso di essermi rotto/a...
pensoh dee essermee rottoh/ah

Do I need...

Ho bisogno di...
oh beezonyo dee

...an injection?

...un'iniezione?
ooneenyetsyoneh

...an operation?

...un'operazione?
oonoperatsyoneh

Will it hurt?

Sarà doloroso/a?
sarah dolorozoh/ah

How long will it take?

Quanto tempo sarà necessario?
kwantoh tempoh sarah nechessaryo

What are the visiting hours?

Quali sono gli orari di visita?
kwalee sonoh lyee oraree dee veezeetah

la rianimazione
lah reeaneematsyoneh
resuscitation

la sedia a rotelle
lah sedya ah rotelleh
wheelchair

la stecca
lah stekkah
splint

la fasciatura
lah fashyatoorah
dressing

EMERGENCIES

In an emergency, you should dial 112 and ask for either an ambulance (*un ambulanza*), the fire department (*i vigili del fuoco*), the police (*la Polizia*), or the military police (*i Carabinieri*), which is part of the army. If you are the victim of a crime or lose your passport or money, you should report the incident to the police. In the following pages, you will find some useful phrases to help you.

IN AN EMERGENCY

Help!	Aiuto! *ayewtoh*
Please go away!	Mi lasci stare! *mee lashee stareh*
Let go!	Lasci! *lashee*
Stop! Thief!	Fermo! Al ladro! *fermoh al ladroh*
Call the police!	Chiamate la polizia! *kiamateh lah poleetseeya*
Get a doctor!	Trovate un dottore! *trovateh oon dottoreh*
I need...	Ho bisogno... *oh beezonyo*
...the police	...della polizia *dellah poleetseeya*
...the fire department	...dei vigili del fuoco *day veejeelee del fwoko*
...an ambulance	...di un'ambulanza *dee oon amboolantsa*
It's very urgent	È molto urgente *eh moltoh oorjenteh*
Where is...	Dov'è... *doveh*
...the American/British embassy?	...l'ambasciata americana/brittanica? *lambashyatah amereekanah/breetaneekah*
...the police station?	...il commissariato? *eel komeesareeyatoh*
...the hospital?	...l'ospedale? *lospedaleh*

EMERGENCIES

ACCIDENTS

I need to make a telephone call	Devo fare una telefonata
devoh fareh oonah telefonatah
I'd like to report an accident	Vorrei denunciare un incidente
vorray denoonchyareh oon eencheedenteh
I've crashed my car	Ho avuto un incidente d'auto
oh avootoh oon eencheedenteh dowtoh
The registration number is...	Il numero di targa è...
eel noomeroh dee targah eh
I'm at...	Mi trovo a/in...
mee trovoh ah/een
Please come quickly!	Venite subito, per favore!
veneeteh soobeetoh pehr favoreh
Someone's injured	Qualcuno è ferito
kwalkoonoh eh fereetoh
Someone's been knocked down	Qualcuno è stato investito
kwalkoonoh eh statoh eenvesteetoh
There's a fire at...	C'è un incendio a/in...
che oon eenchendyo ah/een

YOU MAY HEAR...

Di quale servizio ha bisogno?
dee kwaleh serveetsyo ah beezonyo
Which service do you require?

Cos'è successo?
kozeh sootchessoh
What happened?

EMERGENCY SERVICES

l'idrante
leedranteh
fire hydrant

i vigili del fuoco
ee veejeelee del fwoko
firefighters

l'estintore
lesteentoreh
fire extinguisher

la volante
lah volanteh
police car

le manette
leh manetteh
handcuffs

l'allarme antincendio
lalarmeh anteenchendyo
fire alarm

il poliziotto
eel poleetsyottoh
police officer

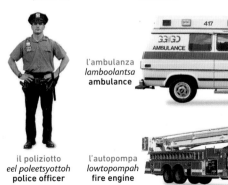

l'ambulanza
lamboolantsa
ambulance

l'autopompa
lowtopompah
fire engine

POLICE AND CRIME

I want to report a crime	Desidero sporgere denuncia
	deseederoh sporjereh denoonchya
I've been...	Sono vittima...
	sonoh veeteemah
...robbed	...di un furto
	dee oon foortoh
...attacked	...di un attacco
	dee oon attakko
...mugged	...di un borseggio
	dee oon borsedjoh
...raped	...di una violenza sessuale
	dee oonah vyolentsa sessooaleh
...burgled	...di un furto
	dee oon foortoh
Someone has stolen...	Qualcuno ha rubato...
	kwalkoonoh ah roobatoh
...my car	...la mia auto
	lah meeah owtoh
...my money	...il mio denaro
	eel meeoh denaroh
...my passport	...il mio passaporto
	eel meeah passaportoh

YOU MAY HEAR...

Quando è successo?
kwandoh eh sootchessoh
When did it happen?

Si ricorda l'aspetto?
see reekordah laspettoh
What did he look like?

Ci sono
testimoni?
*chee sonoh
testeemonee*
**Was there a
witness?**

I'd like to speak to...	Vorrei parlare con... *vorray parlareh kon*
...a senior officer	...un responsabile *oon responsabeeleh*
...a policewoman	...una poliziotta *oonah poleetsyottah*
I need...	Ho bisogno di... *oh beezonyo dee*
...a lawyer	...un avvocato *oon avokatoh*
...an interpreter	...un interprete *oon eenterpreteh*
...to make a phone call	...fare una telefonata *fareh oonah telefonatah*
I'm very sorry, officer	Mi spiace molto, signor agente *mee spyacheh moltoh seenyor ajenteh*
Here is...	Ecco... *ekko*
...my driver's license	...la patente *lah patenteh*
...my insurance	...l'assicurazione *lasseekooratsyoneh*
How much is the fine?	A quanto ammonta la multa? *ah kwantoh ammontah lah mooltah*

YOU MAY HEAR...

Favorisca la patente per favore
favoreeska lah patenteh pehr favoreh
Your license please

Favorisca i documenti
favoreeska ee dokomentee
Your papers

AT THE GARAGE

🎧

Where is the nearest garage?	Dov'è la più vicina autofficina? *doveh lah pew veecheenah owtoffeecheenah*
Can you do repairs?	Effettuate le riparazioni? *effettwateh leh reeparatsyonee*
I need...	Ho bisogno di... *oh beezonyo dee*
...a new tire	...un nuovo pneumatico *oon nwovoh pneoomateekoh*
...a new exhaust	...un nuovo tubo di scarico *oon nwovoh tooboh dee skareekoh*
...a new windshield	...un nuovo parabrezza *oon nwovoh parabretsa*
...a new headlight	...una nuova lampadina *oonah nwovah lampadeenah*
...wiper blades	...spazzole del tergicristallo *spatsoleh del terjeekreestalloh*
Do you have one in stock?	Ne avete in magazzino? *neh aveteh een magadzeenoh*
Can you replace this?	Può sostituirlo/a? *pwo sosteetweerloh/ah*
The...is not working	Il/la...non funziona *eel/lah...non foontsyonah*
There is something wrong with the engine	Il motore non funziona bene *eel motoreh non foontsyonah beneh*
Is it serious?	È grave? *eh graveh*
When will it be ready?	Quando sarà pronta? *kwandoh sarah prontah*
How much will it cost?	Quanto costerà? *kwantoh kosterah*

CAR BREAKDOWN

My car has broken down	La mia automobile è in panne *lah meeah owtomobeeleh eh een panneh*
Please can you help me?	Mi può aiutare? *mee pwo ayewtareh*
Please come to...	Venga a... *vengah ah*
I have a flat tire	Ho una gomma a terra *oh oonah gommah ah terrah*
Can you help change the wheel?	Mi può aiutare a cambiare la ruota? *mee pwo ayewtareh ah kambyareh lah rwotah*
I need a new tire	Ho bisogno di un nuovo pneumatico *oh beezonyo dee oon nwovoh pneoomateekoh*
My car won't start	La mia auto non si accende *lah meeah owtoh non see atchendeh*
The engine is overheating	Il motore si sta surriscaldando *eel motoreh see stah sooreeskaldandoh*
Can you fix it?	Può aggiustarla? *pwo adjoostarlah*

YOU MAY HEAR...

Ha bisogno di aiuto?
ah beezonyo dee ayewtoh
Do you need any help?

Qual è il problema?
kwaleh eel problemah
What is the problem?

Ha la ruota di scorta?
ah lah rwotah dee skortah
Do you have a spare tire?

LOST PROPERTY

I've lost...
Ho smarrito...
oh smareetoh

...my money
...il mio denaro
eel meeoh denaroh

...my keys
...le chiavi
leh kyavee

...my glasses
...gli occhiali
lyee okyalee

My luggage is missing
Il mio bagaglio è smarrito
eel meeoh bagalyo eh smareetoh

My suitcase has been damaged
La mia valigia è stata danneggiata
la meeah valeeja eh statah dannedjatah

il portafoglio
eel portafolyoh
wallet

il passaporto
eel passaportoh
passport

la carta di credito
lah kartah dee kredeetoh
credit card

il portamonete
eel portamoneteh
change purse

la fotocamera
lah fotokamerah
camera

lo smartphone
loh smartphone
smartphone

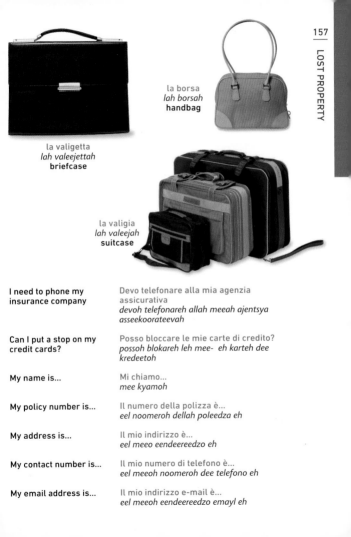

la valigetta
lah valeejettah
briefcase

la borsa
lah borsah
handbag

la valigia
lah valeejah
suitcase

I need to phone my insurance company	Devo telefonare alla mia agenzia assicurativa *devoh telefonareh allah meeah ajentsya asseekoorateevah*
Can I put a stop on my credit cards?	Posso bloccare le mie carte di credito? *possoh blokareh leh mee- eh karteh dee kredeetoh*
My name is...	Mi chiamo... *mee kyamoh*
My policy number is...	Il numero della polizza è... *eel noomeroh dellah poleedza eh*
My address is...	Il mio indirizzo è... *eel meeo eendeereedzo eh*
My contact number is...	Il mio numero di telefono è... *eel meeoh noomeroh dee telefono eh*
My email address is...	Il mio indirizzo e-mail è... *eel meeoh eendeereedzo emayl eh*

MENU GUIDE

This guide lists the most common terms you may encounter on Italian menus or when shopping for food. If you can't find an exact phrase, try looking up its component parts.

A

abbacchio alla romana *Roman-style spring lamb*
acciughe sott'olio *anchovies in oil*
aceto *vinegar*
acqua *water*
acqua minerale gassata *sparkling mineral water*
acqua minerale non gassata *still mineral water*
acqua naturale *still mineral water, tap water*
affettato misto *variety of cold, sliced meats*
affogato al caffè *hot espresso on ice cream*
aglio *garlic*
agnello *lamb*
albicocche *apricots*
al forno *roast*
amatriciana *chopped bacon and tomato sauce*
ananas *pineapple*
anatra *duck*
anatra all'arancia *duck in orange sauce*
anguilla in umido *stewed eel*
anguria *watermelon*
antipasti *appetizers*
antipasti misti *mixed appetizers*
aperitivo *aperitif*
aragosta *lobster*

arancia *orange*
aranciata *orangeade; fresh orange juice*
aringa *herring*
arrosto *roast*
arrosto di tacchino *roast turkey*
asparagi *asparagus*
avocado all'agro *avocado with dressing*

B

baccalà *dried cod*
baccalà alla vicentina *Vicentine-style dried cod*
bagnacauda *vegetables (often raw) in a sauce of oil, garlic, and anchovy*
Barbaresco *dry red wine from Piedmont*
Barbera *dry red wine from Piedmont*
Bardolino *dry red wine from the Veneto region*
Barolo *dark, dry red wine from Piedmont*
basilico *basil*
bavarese *ice-cream cake; dessert made with cream*
Bel Paese *soft, white cheese*
besciamella *white sauce*
bignè *cream puff*
birra *beer*
birra chiara *light beer, lager*

birra grande *large beer*
birra piccola *small beer*
birra scura *dark beer*
bistecca ai ferri *grilled steak*
bistecca (di manzo) *steak*
bolognese *mince and tomato sauce*
braciola di maiale *pork steak*
branzino al forno *baked sea bass*
brasato *braised beef with herbs*
bresaola *dried, salted beef eaten with oil and lemon*
brioche *type of croissant*
brodo *clear broth*
brodo vegetale *clear vegetable broth*
bucatini *long tube pasta*
budino *pudding*
burro *butter*
burro di acciughe *anchovy butter*

C

Caciotta *tender, white cheese from Central Italy*
caffè *coffee*
caffè corretto *espresso with a dash of liqueur*
caffè latte *half coffee, half hot milk*
caffè lungo *weak espresso*
caffè macchiato *espresso with a dash of milk*
caffè ristretto *strong espresso*
calamari in umido *stewed squid*
calamaro *squid*
calzone *folded pizza with tomato and cheese*
camomilla *chamomile tea*
cannella *cinnamon*
cannelloni al forno *baked pasta rolls filled with meat*

cappuccino *espresso with frothy milk sprinkled with cocoa powder*
capretto al forno *roast kid*
carbonara *sauce of egg, bacon, and cheese*
carciofi *artichokes*
carciofini sott'olio *baby artichokes in oil*
carne *meat*
carote *carrots*
carpaccio *finely sliced beef fillet with oil, lemon, and parmesan*
carré di maiale al forno *roast pork loin*
cassata siciliana *ice-cream cake with chocolate, glacé fruit, and ricotta*
castagne *chestnuts*
cavoletti di Bruxelles *Brussels sprouts*
cavolfiore *cauliflower*
cavolo *cabbage*
cefalo *grey mullet*
cernia *grouper (fish)*
cetriolo *cucumber*
charlotte *ice-cream cake with biscuits and fruit*
Chianti *dark red Tuscan wine*
cicoria *chicory*
cicorino *small chicory plants*
ciliege *cherries*
cime di rapa *sprouting broccoli*
cioccolata *chocolate*
cioccolata calda *hot chocolate*
cipolle *onions*
cocktail di gamberetti *shrimp cocktail*
conchiglie alla marchigiana *pasta shells in tomato sauce with ham, celery, carrot, and parsley*
coniglio *rabbit*

coniglio in umido *stewed rabbit*

consommé *clear broth*

contorni *vegetables*

coperto *cover charge*

coppa *cured neck of pork*

costata alla fiorentina *T-bone veal steak*

costata di manzo *T-bone beef steak*

cotechino *spiced pork sausage for boiling*

cotoletta *veal, pork, or lamb chop*

cotoletta ai ferri *grilled veal or pork chop*

cotoletta alla milanese *veal chop in breadcrumbs*

cotoletta alla valdostana *veal chop with ham and cheese, in breadcrumbs*

cotolette di agnello *lamb chops*

cotolette di maiale *pork chops*

cozze *mussels*

cozze alla marinara *mussels in white wine*

crema *custard dessert made with eggs and milk*

crema al caffè *coffee custard dessert*

crema al cioccolato *chocolate custard dessert*

crema di funghi *cream of mushroom soup*

crema di piselli *cream of pea soup*

crema pasticciera *confectioner's custard*

crêpes Suzette *crêpes flambéed with orange sauce*

crescente *fried bread made with flour, lard, and eggs*

crespelle *savoury crêpes*

crostata di frutta *fruit tart*

D, E

dadi *bouillon cubes*

datteri *dates*

degustazione di vini *wine tasting*

dentice al forno *baked dentex (type of sea bream)*

digestivo *digestive liqueur*

Dolcelatte *creamy blue cheese*

dolci *sweets, desserts, cakes*

endivia belga *white chicory*

entrecôte (di manzo) *beef entrecote*

espresso *strong, black coffee*

F

fagiano *pheasant*

fagioli *beans*

fagioli borlotti in umido *borlotti beans in tomatoes and vegetables*

fagiolini *long, green beans*

faraona *guinea fowl*

farcito *stuffed*

fegato *liver*

fegato alla veneta *liver in butter with onions*

fegato con salvia e burro *liver in butter and sage*

fettuccine *ribbon-shaped pasta*

fichi *figs*

filetti di pesce persico *fillets of perch*

filetti di sogliola *fillets of sole*

filetto ai ferri *grilled fillet of beef*

filetto al cognac *fillet of beef flambé*

filetto al pepe verde *fillet of beef with green peppercorns*

filetto al sangue *rare fillet of beef*

filetto ben cotto *well-done fillet of beef*

filetto (di manzo) *fillet of beef*

filetto medio *medium-cooked fillet of beef*
finocchi gratinati *fennel au gratin*
finocchio *fennel*
fonduta *cheese fondue*
formaggi misti *variety of cheeses*
fragole *strawberries*
fragole con gelato/panna *strawberries and ice cream/cream*
frappé *fruit or milk shake with crushed ice*
Frascati *dry white wine from area around Rome*
frittata *type of omelet*
frittata alle erbe *herb omelet*
fritto *deep fried*
fritto misto *mixed seafood in batter*
frittura di pesce *variety of fried fish*
frutta *fruit*
frutta alla fiamma *fruit flambé*
frutta secca *dried nuts and raisins*
frutti di bosco *mixture of strawberries, raspberries, mulberries, etc*
frutti di mare *seafood*
funghi *mushrooms*
funghi trifolati *mushrooms fried in garlic and parsley*

G

gamberetti *shrimps*
gamberi *prawns*
gamberoni *king prawns*
gazzosa *clear lemonade*
gelatina *jelly*
gelato *ice cream*
gelato di crema *vanilla-flavored ice cream*

gelato di frutta *fruit-flavored ice cream*
gnocchetti verdi agli spinaci e al gorgonzola *small flour, potato, and spinach dumplings with melted gorgonzola*
gnocchi *small flour and potato dumplings*
gnocchi alla romana *small milk and semolina dumplings with butter*
Gorgonzola *strong blue cheese from Lombardy*
grancevola *spiny spider crab*
granchio *crab*
granita *sherbet made of sweetened syrup*
grigliata di pesce *grilled fish*
grigliata mista *mixed grill (meat or fish)*
grissini *thin, crisp breadsticks*
Gruviera *Gruyère cheese*

I

indivia *endive*
insalata *salad*
insalata caprese *salad of tomatoes and mozzarella*
insalata di funghi porcini *boletus mushroom salad*
insalata di mare *seafood salad*
insalata di nervetti *boiled beef or veal tendons served cold with beans and pickles*
insalata di pomodori *tomato salad*
insalata di riso *rice salad*
insalata mista *mixed salad*
insalata russa *Russian salad*
insalata verde *green salad*
involtini *meat rolls stuffed with ham and herbs*

L

lamponi *raspberries*
lasagne al forno *layers of pasta baked in meat sauce with cheese*
latte *milk*
latte macchiato con cioccolato *hot milk sprinkled with cocoa*
lattuga *lettuce*
leggero *light*
legumi *legumes or pulses*
lemonsoda *sparkling lemon drink*
lenticchie *lentils*
lepre *hare*
limonata *lemon-flavored fizzy drink*
limone *lemon*
lingua *tongue*

M

macedonia di frutta *fruit salad*
maiale *pork*
maionese *mayonnaise*
mandarino *mandarin*
mandorla *almond*
manzo *beef*
marroni *large chestnuts*
Marsala *fortified wine*
marzapane *marzipan*
Mascarpone *soft, mild cheese*
medaglioni di vitello *veal medallions*
mela *apple*
melagrana *pomegranate*
melanzane *eggplant*
melone *melon*
menta *mint*
meringata *meringue pie*
merluzzo *cod*
merluzzo alla pizzaiola *cod in tomato sauce with anchovies and capers*
merluzzo in bianco *cod with oil and lemon*

messicani in gelatina *rolls of veal in jelly*
millefoglie *pastry layered with custard*
minestra in brodo *noodle soup*
minestrone *vegetable soup with rice or pasta*
mirtilli *bilberries*
more *mulberries or blackberries*
moscato *sweet wine*
mousse al cioccolato *chocolate mousse*
Mozzarella *soft cheese*
mozzarella in carrozza *fried slices of bread and mozzarella*

N, O

nasello *hake*
nocciole *hazelnuts*
noce moscata *nutmeg*
noci *walnuts*
nodino *veal chop*
olio *oil*
origano *oregano*
ossobuco *stewed shin of veal*
ostriche *oysters*

P

paglia e fieno *mixed plain and green tagliatelle*
paillard di manzo *slices of grilled beef*
paillard di vitello *slices of grilled veal*
pane *bread*
panino *filled roll; bread roll*
panna *cream*
parmigiana di melanzane *eggplant baked with cheese*
pasta al forno *pasta baked in white sauce with grated cheese*
pasta e fagioli *thick soup with borlotti beans and pasta rings*

pasta e piselli *pasta with peas*

pasticcio di fegato d'oca *baked pasta dish with goose liver*

pasticcio di lepre *baked pasta dish with hare*

pasticcio di maccheroni *baked macaroni*

pastina in brodo *soup with small pasta*

patate *potatoes*

patate al forno/arrosto *roast potatoes*

patate fritte *French fries*

patate in insalata *potato salad*

Pecorino *strong, hard cheese made from sheep's milk*

penne *pasta quills*

penne ai quattro formaggi *pasta with four cheeses sauce*

penne all'arrabbiata *pasta with tomato and chilli pepper sauce*

penne panna e prosciutto *pasta with cream and ham sauce*

pepe *pepper (spice)*

peperoncino *crushed chili pepper*

peperoni *peppers*

peperoni ripieni *stuffed peppers*

peperoni sott'olio *peppers in oil*

pera *pear*

pesca *peach*

pesce *fish*

pesce al cartoccio *fish baked in foil with herbs*

pesce in carpione *marinaded fish*

pesto *sauce of basil, pine nuts, Parmesan, garlic, and oil*

Pinot *dry white wine from the Veneto region*

pinzimonio *sauce with oil and vinegar served with raw vegetables*

piselli *peas*

piselli al prosciutto *peas with ham and basil*

pizzaiola *slices of cooked beef in tomato sauce, oregano, and anchovies*

pizzoccheri alla Valtellinese *pasta strips with vegetables and cheese*

polenta *boiled cornmeal left to set and sliced*

polenta e osei *polenta with small birds*

polenta pasticciata *layers of polenta, tomato sauce, and cheese*

pollo *chicken*

pollo alla cacciatora *chicken in white wine with onions and carrots*

pollo alla diavola *deep-fried chicken pieces*

polpette *meatballs*

polpettone *meatloaf*

pomodori *tomatoes*

pomodori ripieni *stuffed tomatoes*

pompelmo *grapefruit*

porri *leeks*

prezzemolo *parsley*

primi piatti *first courses*

prosciutto cotto *cooked ham*

prosciutto crudo *type of cured ham*

prugne *plums*

punte di asparagi all'agro *asparagus tips in oil and lemon*

purè di patate *mashed potatoes*

puttanesca *tomato sauce with anchovies, capers, and black olives*

Q, R

quaglie *quails*
radicchio *red chicory*
ragù *meat-based sauce*
rapanelli *radishes*
ravioli *stuffed pasta parcels*
ravioli al pomodoro *meat ravioli in tomato sauce*
razza *skate*
Ricotta *type of cottage cheese*
risi e bisi *risotto with peas and ham*
riso *rice*
risotto *rice cooked in stock*
risotto alla castellana *risotto with mushroom, ham, cream, and cheese*
risotto alla milanese *risotto with saffron*
risotto al nero di seppia *risotto with cuttlefish ink*
risotto al tartufo *truffle risotto*
roast-beef all'inglese *thinly sliced cold roast beef*
Robiola *type of soft cheese from Lombardy*
rognone trifolato *kidney in garlic, oil, and parsley*
rosatello/rosato *rosé wine*
rosmarino *rosemary*

S

salame *salami*
sale *salt*
salmone affumicato *smoked salmon*
salsa cocktail/rosa *mayonnaise and ketchup sauce for fish and seafood*
salsa di pomodoro *tomato sauce*

salsa tartara *tartar sauce*
salsa vellutata *white sauce made with clear broth*
salsa verde *sauce for meat, with parsley and oil*
salsiccia *sausage*
salsiccia di cinghiale *wild boar sausage*
salsiccia di maiale *pork sausage*
saltimbocca alla romana *slices of veal stuffed with ham and sage and fried*
salvia *sage*
sambuca (con la mosca) *aniseed-flavor liqueur served with a coffee bean*
sarde ai ferri *grilled sardines*
scaloppine *veal escalopes*
scaloppine al prezzemolo *veal escalopes with parsley*
scamorza alla griglia *grilled soft cheese*
scampi alla griglia *grilled scampi*
secco *dry*
secondi piatti *second courses, main courses*
sedano *celery*
selvaggina *game*
semifreddo *cake or dessert often containing cream and served chilled*
senape *mustard*
seppie in umido *stewed cuttlefish*
servizio compreso *service charge included*
servizio escluso *service charge not included*
Soave *dry white wine from the Veneto region*
sogliola *sole*
sogliola ai ferri *grilled sole*

sogliola al burro *sole cooked in butter*
sogliola alla mugnaia *sole cooked in flour and butter*
sorbetto *sorbet, soft ice cream*
soufflé al formaggio *cheese soufflé*
soufflé al prosciutto *ham soufflé*
speck *cured, smoked ham*
spezzatino di vitello *veal stew*
spiedini *assorted chunks of spit-cooked meat or fish*
spinaci *spinach*
spinaci all'agro *spinach with oil and lemon*
spremuta di... *freshly squeezed...juice*
spumante *sparkling wine*
Stracchino *soft cheese from Lombardy*
stracciatella *soup of beaten eggs in clear broth*
strudel di mele *apple strudel*
stufato *braised*
succo di... *...juice*
sugo al tonno *tomato sauce with tuna, garlic, and parsley*

T

tacchino ripieno *stuffed turkey*
tagliata *finely cut beef fillet cooked in the oven*
tagliatelle *thin ribbon-shaped pasta*
tagliatelle rosse *tagliatelle made with beetroot*
tagliatelle verdi *tagliatelle made with spinach*
tagliolini *thin soup noodles*
tartine *small sandwiches*
tartufo *ice cream covered in cocoa or chocolate; truffle*

tè *tea*
tiramisù *dessert with coffee-soaked sponge, Marsala, Mascarpone, and cocoa powder*
tonno *tuna*
torta *tart, flan*
torta di ricotta *type of cheesecake*
torta salata *savoury flan*
tortellini *pasta shapes filled with minced pork, ham, Parmesan, and nutmeg*
trancio di palombo *smooth dogfish steak*
trancio di pesce spada *swordfish steak*
trenette col pesto *flat spaghetti with pesto sauce*
triglia *mullet (fish)*
trippa *tripe*
trota *trout*
trota affumicata *smoked trout*
trota al burro *trout cooked in butter*
trota alle mandorle *trout with almonds*
trota bollita *boiled trout*

U

uccelletti *small birds wrapped in bacon, served on cocktail sticks*
uova *eggs*
uova alla coque *soft-boiled eggs*
uova al tegamino con pancetta *fried eggs and bacon*
uova farcite *eggs with tuna, capers, and mayonnaise filling*
uova sode *hard-boiled eggs*
uva *grapes*
uva bianca *white grapes*
uva nera *black grapes*

MENU GUIDE

V

vellutata di asparagi
*creamed asparagus with
egg yolks*
vellutata di piselli
*creamed peas with
egg yolks*
verdura *vegetables*
vermicelli *long,
very fine, thin pasta*
vino *wine*
vino bianco
white wine
vino da dessert
dessert wine
vino da pasto *table wine*
vino da tavola *table wine*
vino rosso *red wine*
vitello *veal*
vitello tonnato *cold sliced
veal in tuna, anchovy, oil,
and lemon sauce*
vongole *clams*

W, Z

würstel *hot dog*
zabaglione *creamy dessert
of eggs, sugar, and Marsala*
zafferano *saffron*
zucca *pumpkin*
zucchero *sugar*
zucchine *zucchini*
zucchine al pomodoro
*zucchini in tomato, garlic,
and parsley sauce*
zucchine ripiene
stuffed zucchini
zuccotto *ice-cream cake
with sponge fingers, cream,
and chocolate*
zuppa *soup*
zuppa di cipolle *onion soup*
zuppa di cozze *mussel soup*
zuppa di lenticchie *lentil soup*
zuppa di pesce *fish soup*
zuppa di verdura *vegetable soup*
zuppa inglese *trifle*

The gender of an Italian noun is shown by the word for "the": **il** or **lo** (masculine), **la** (feminine), and their plural forms **i** or **gli** (masculine) and **le** (feminine). When **lo** or **la** are abbreviated to **l'** in front of a vowel or h, the gender of the noun is shown by the abbreviation **(m)** or **(f)** after it.

A

a little *un poco*
a lot *molto*
about *circa*
above *sopra*
accident *l'incidente (m)*
accident and emergency
  il Pronto Soccorso
accommodation *alloggio*
account number
  il numero di conto
across *attraverso*
activities *le attività (f)*
actor *l'attore (m)*
actress *l'attrice (f)*
adapter *l'adattatore (m)*
add (verb) *sommare*
address *l'indirizzo (m)*
adhesive bandage *il cerotto*
adhesive tape *lo scotch*
adult *l'adulto (m)*
aerobics *l'aerobica (f)*
after *dopo*
afternoon *il pomeriggio*
aftersun *il doposole (m)*
again *ancora*
air-conditioning
  l'aria condizionata (f)
airmail *la posta aerea*
airplane *l'aeroplano (m)*
airport *l'aeroporto (m)*
aisle *la corsia (f)*
aisle seat *il posto*

  vicino al corridoio
alarm clock *la sveglia (f)*
alcoholic drinks
  le bevande alcoliche (f)
all *tutto*
allergic *allergico/a*
allergy *l'allergia (f)*
almost *quasi*
alone *solo/a*
along *lungo*
already *già*
altitude *la quota*
always *sempre*
ambulance
  l'ambulanza (f)
amount *l'importo (m)*
and *e*
angry *arrabbiato/a*
animals *gli animali*
ankle *la caviglia*
another *altro/a*
answering machine
  la segreteria telefonica
answer (verb) *rispondere*
antibiotics *gli antibiotici*
antiseptic *il disinfettante (m)*
anything *niente; qualcosa*
apartment block
  il condominio (m)
appearance *l'aspetto (m)*
appetizer *l'antipasto*
applaud (verb) *applaudire*
apple *la mela (f)*

apple juice
  il succo di mela (m)
application *l'applicazione (f)*
appointment
  l'appuntamento (m)
apricot *l'albicocca (f)*
April *aprile*
apron *il grembiule*
arc *l'arco (m)*
arch *l'arco plantare (m)*
architect *l'architetto (m)*
architecture
  l'archittettura (f)
area *la superficie (f)*
arm *il braccio*
around *attorno*
arrangements
  gli accordi
arrivals hall *gli arrivi*
arrive (verb) *arrivare*
art *l'arte (f)*
art gallery *la galleria d'arte*
arthritis *l'artrite (f)*
artificial sweetener
  il dolcificante
artist *l'artista (f)*
as *come*
ashtray *il posacenere (m)*
assistant *l'assistente (m/f)*
asthma *l'asma (f)*
at *a*
athlete *l'atleta (m)*
ATM *il bancomat (m)*
attachment *l'allegato (m)*
attack *l'attacco (m)*
attend (verb) *partecipare*
attractions
  i luoghi d'interesse (m)
audience *il pubblico (m)*
audio guide *l'audio guida*
August *agosto*
aunt *la zia (f)*
Australia *Australia (f)*

automatic *automatico*
automatic payment *l'addebito
  diretto (m)*
automatic ticket machine
  la biglietteria automatica
avenue *il viale (m)*
avocado *l'avocado (m)*
awful *orribile*

B

baby *il bimbo (m)*
baby changing room
  lo spazio con fasciatoio (m)
babysitting
  il servizio di babysitting
back (body) *la schiena*
back (not front of) *la parte
  posteriore*
backpack *lo zaino*
bacon *la pancetta (f)*
bad *cattivo/a*
badminton *il volano*
bag *la borsa*
bagel *il bagel*
baggage allowance
  il bagaglio consentito
baggage claim
  il ritiro bagagli
baguette *il filone*
baker *la panetteria*
bakery *il panificio*
bake (verb) *cuocere al forno*
balcony *il balcone*
ball *la palla*
ballet *la danza*
banana *la banana*
bandage *la benda*
bank *la banca*
bank account *il conto bancario*
bank charge
  la commissione bancaria
bank transfer *il bonifico*
bar *il bar*

barbecue
  la griglia per barbecue
barber *il barbiere*
bar snacks *gli stuzzichini*
bartender *il barista*
baseball glove
  il guanto da baseball
basement *il seminterrato*
basil *il basilico*
basket *il cestino*
basketball *la palla da basket*
bath robe *l'accappatoio (m)*
bathroom *il bagno*
bath towel
  l'asciugamano grande (m)
bathtub *la vasca*
battery *la batteria*
beach *la spiaggia*
beach ball
  il pallone da spiaggia
beach towel
  il telo da spiaggia
beans *i chicchi*
bear *l'orso (m)*
beautiful *bello/a*
bed *il letto*
bed and breakfast
  la pensione con colazione
bed linen *la biancheria da letto*
bedroom *la camera da letto*
bee *l'ape (f)*
beef *il manzo*
beer *la birra*
beet *la barbabietola*
beetle *il coleottero*
before *prima di*
beginner
  principiante (m/f)
beginning *l'inizio*
behind *dietro a*
bell *il campanello*
below *sotto*
belt *la cintura*

bench *la panca*
beneath *sotto*
berry *la bacca*
beside *vicino a*
better *migliore*
between *tra*
be (verb) *essere*
beyond *oltre*
bicycle *la bicicletta*
big *grande*
bike rack *il cavalletto*
bikini *il bikini*
bill (note) *la nota*
birds *gli uccelli*
birth *la nascita*
birth certificate
  il certificato di nascita
birthday *il compleanno*
bite *il morso*
bitter *amaro*
black *nero/a*
black coffee *il caffè nero*
black tea *il tè nero*
blackberry *la mora*
blackcurrant *il ribes nero*
blanket *la coperta*
bleach *la candeggina*
blender *il frullatore*
blister *la vescica*
block *la parata*
blonde *biondo*
blood pressure
  la pressione sanguigna
blood test *le analisi del sangue*
blouse *la camicetta*
blow dry (verb)
  asciugare con il fon
blow-dryer *l'asciugacapelli (m)*
blue *blu*
blueberry *il mirtillo*
blush *il fard*
board (verb) *imbarcarsi*
boarding gate

l'uscita d'imbarco (f)
boarding pass
  la carta d'imbarco
boat la barca
body il corpo
body lotion
  la crema per il corpo
boil (verb) bollire
book il libro
book (verb) prenotare
book a flight (verb)
  prenotare un volo
bookstore la libreria
boot lo stivale
bored annoiato
borrow (verb) prendere
  in prestito
bottle la bottiglia
bottle opener
  l'apribottiglie (m)
bottled water l'acqua in
  bottiglia (f)
boutique la boutique
bowl la scodella
bowling il bowling
box la scatola
box office la biglietteria
boy il ragazzo
boyfriend il fidanzato
bracelet il braccale
brain il cervello
brake il freno
branch il ramo
bread il pane
breakdown il guasto
breakfast la colazione
breakfast buffet
  il buffet della colazione
breakfast cereals
  i cereali da colazione
brick il mattone
bridge il dorso
  del piede

briefcase la valigetta
briefs lo slip
brioche la brioche
British britannico/a
broccoli il broccolo
broil (verb) cuocere
  alla griglia
broken rotto/a
broom la scopa
brother il fratello
brown marrone
brown rice il riso integrale
browse (verb) navigare
bruise l'ematoma (m)
brunette bruno
brush la spazzola
brush (cleaning) la scopa
bubblebath il bagnoschiuma
bucket il secchio
buckle la fibbia
buffet il buffet
build (verb) costruire
bulb il bulbo
bulletin board il tabellone
bumper il paraurti
bun la pastina
bunch il mazzetto
buoy la boa
burger l'hamburger (m)
burgle (verb) svaligiare
burn la bruciatura
bus l'autobus (m)
bus driver l'autista
bus station la stazione
  degli autobus
bus stop la fermata
  dell'autobus
bus ticket il biglietto
business, on per lavoro
bust il busto
butcher la macelleria
butter il burro
butternut squash

la zucca Butternut
button *il bottone*
buy (verb) *comprare*
by *da; vicino a*

C

cab *taxi*
cabin *la cabina*
cable *il cavo*
cable car *la funivia*
cable television
  la televisione via cavo
café *il bar*
cakes *i dolci*
calculator *la calcolatrice*
calendar *il calendario*
call button *il pulsante*
  di chiamata
calm *calmo/a*
camera *la fotocamera*
camera bag *la borsa*
  per fotocamera
camera case *la custodia*
camisole *il corpetto*
camp (verb) *campeggiare*
camper van *il camper*
camping kettle *il bollitore*
camping stove *il fornetto*
  da campeggio
campsite *il campeggio*
Canada *il Canada*
can (noun) *la scatoletta*
can (verb) *potere*
candy *le caramelle*
canoe *la canoa*
can opener *l'apribottiglie (m)*
cap *la cuffia*
capital *la capitale*
cappuccino *il cappuccino*
capsule *la capsula*
car *la macchina*
car accident
  l'incidente stradale

card *il biglietto d'auguri*
cardboard *il cartone*
cardigan *il cardigan*
cards *le carte*
car rental *l'autonoleggio (m)*
car rental desk *l'ufficio*
  dell'autonoleggio (m)
cart *il carrello*
car wash *l'autolavaggio*
carnival *il carnevale*
carpet *il tappeto*
carrot *la carota*
carry (verb) *portare*
carton *il cartone*
case *la custodia*
cash *il denaro*
cash machine
  il sportello bancomat
cash register *la cassa*
cash (verb) *riscuotere*
casino *il casinò*
casserole dish *la casseruola*
castle *il castello*
casual *casual*
cat *il gatto*
catamaran *il catamarano*
catch (verb) *prendere*
cathedral *la cattedrale*
cauliflower *il cavolfiore*
caution *attenzione*
cave *la caverna*
CD *il CD*
ceiling *il soffitto*
celebration *la festa*
cell phone *il cellulare*
central heating
  il riscaldamento centralizzato
center *il centro*
cereal *il cereale*
chair *la sedia*
chair lift *la seggiovia*
champagne *lo champagne*
change (verb) *cambiare*

change purse *il portamonete*
channel *il canale*
channel (TV) *il canale*
charge *l'imputazione (f)*
charge (verb) *addebitare*
chart *la scheda del paziente*
check *il conto*
check *l'assegno (m)*
checkbook *il libretto*
check card *la carta assegni*
checker *il cassiere*
check in *il check-in*
check in (verb) *fare il check-in*
check-in desk *il banco accettazione*
checking account *il conto corrente*
check out (hotel) *lasciare*
checkout (supermarket) *la cassa*
checkup *il controllo*
cheek *la guancia*
cheers! *cin cin!*
cheese *il formaggio*
chef *il cuoco*
cherry *la ciliegia*
cherry tomato *il pomodoro ciliegino*
chest *il torace*
chewing gum *la gomma da masticare*
chicken *il pollo*
chickpeas *i ceci*
child *bambino/a (m/f)*
children *i bambini*
chili pepper *il peperoncino*
chill *l'infreddatura (f)*
chin *il mento*
chocolate *il cioccolatino*
choke (verb) *soffocare*
chop *la costoletta*
chorizo *il chorizo*
church *la chiesa*

cigar *il sigaro*
cigarette *la sigaretta*
cigarettes *le sigarette*
cilantro *il coriandolo*
cinnamon *la cannella*
circle *il cerchio*
citrus fruit *gli agrumi*
city *la città*
clam *la vongola*
clean *pulito/a*
client *il cliente*
cliff *la scogliera*
clinic *la clinica*
clock *l'orologio*
clock radio *la radiosveglia*
close (near) *vicino*
close (verb) *chiudere*
closed *chiuso/a*
closet *l'armadio*
clothes *gli abiti*
clothing *l'abbigliamento (m)*
cloud *la nuvola*
cloudy *nuvoloso/a*
club *il fiore*
clubbing *andare in discoteca*
coach *il pullman*
coast *la costa*
coaster *il sottobicchiere*
coast guard *il guardacoste*
coat *il cappotto*
coat hanger *l'appendiabiti (m)*
cockroach *la blatta*
cocktail *il cocktail*
coconut *la noce di cocco*
cod *il merluzzo*
coffee *il caffè*
coffee cup *la tazzina da caffè*
coffee machine *la macchina del caffè*
coffee table *il tavolino*
coin *la moneta*
colander *il colino*

cold *freddo/a*
cold (illness) *il raffreddore*
collect call *la chiamata*
  a carico del destinatario
collection *la collezione*
college *l'università*
colored pencil
  la matita colorata
colors *i colori*
comb *il pettine*
come (verb) *venire*
comforter *il piumone*
comic book *il fumetto*
company *la ditta*
compartment *il scompartimento*
compass *la bussola*
complain (verb) *reclamare*
complaint *la denuncia*
computer *il computer*
concert *il concerto*
concourse *l'atrio (m)*
conditioner *il balsamo*
condom *il preservativo*
confident *sicuro/a di sé*
confused *confuso/a*
connection *la coincidenza*
constipation *la stitichezza*
construction site *il cantiere*
construction worker *il muratore*
consul *il console*
consulate *il consolato*
consultation *la visita*
contact lenses
  le lenti a contatto
contact number
  il numero di telefono
container *il contenitore*
contents *il contenuto*
continent *continente*
contraception
  la contraccezione
cookie *il biscotto*
cookie sheet *la teglia da forno*

cooking *cucinare*
cooler *il frigo portatile*
copy (verb) *copiare*
coral reef *la barriera corallina*
core *il torsolo*
cork *il tappo*
corkscrew *il cavatappi*
corn *il mais*
corner *il calcio d'angolo*
correct *vero/a*
cotton *il cotone*
cough *la tosse*
cough medicine
  la medicina per la tosse
counter *la pedina*
country *il Paese*
count (verb) *contare*
couple *la coppia*
courier *il corriere*
course *il piatto*
courses *le portate*
courtyard *il cortile*
cousin *il cugino*
cow *la mucca*
crab *il granchio*
cramp *il crampo*
cream (lotion) *la crema*
cream cheese
  il formaggio cremoso
crease *la linea*
credit card *la carta di credito*
crêpes *le crêpes*
crib *il lettino*
crime *il reato*
croissant *il cornetto*
cross trainer *l'ellittica (f)*
crushed *tritato/a*
crust *la crosta*
cry (verb) *piangere*
cucumber *il cetriolo*
cufflinks *i gemelli*
cup *la tazza*
curly *riccio*

currency exchange
  l'ufficio di cambio (m)
curry *il curry*
curtain *il sipario*
cushion *il cuscino*
customer *il cliente*
customs *la dogana*
cut *il taglio*
cutlery *le posate*
cycle lane *la pista ciclabile*
cycle (verb) *andare in bici*
cycling helmet *il casco*

D

dairy *i latticini*
damaged *danneggiato/a*
dance *la musica da ballo*
dancing *ballare*
danger *pericolo*
dark *scuro/a*
dashboard *il cruscotto*
daughter *la figlia*
day *il giorno*
day planner *l'agenda (f)*
debit card *la carta di debito*
December *dicembre*
deck chair *la sedia a sdraio*
deep-fried *fritto*
  in olio abbondante
degrees *gradi*
delayed *ritardato/a*
delicatessen *la gastronomia*
delicious *delizioso/a*
delivery *il parto*
dentist *il/la dentista*
deodorant *il deodorante*
department *il dipartimento*
department store
  il grande magazzino
departure board
  il tabellone delle partenze
departure lounge
  la sala delle partenze

departures *le partenze*
departures hall
  le partenze
deposit *il deposito*
desert *il deserto*
desk *la scrivania*
dessert *il dessert*
destination *la destinazione*
detergent *il detergente*
develop (film) *sviluppare*
diabetic *diabetico/a*
dial (verb) *comporre*
diaper *il pannolino*
diarroea *la diarrea*
dictionary *il dizionario*
diesel *il diesel*
difficult *difficile*
digital camera
  la fotocamera digitale
digital radio *la radio digitale*
dining car *la carrozza ristorante*
dining room *la sala da pranzo*
dinner *la cena*
directions *Indicazioni*
dirty *sporco*
disabled parking
  il parcheggio per disabili
discuss (verb) *discutere*
disembark (verb)
  sbarcare
dish *il piatto*
dishwasher *la lavastoviglie*
distance *la distanza*
district *il distretto*
dive (verb) *tuffarsi*
divorced *divorziato/a*
doctor *il dottore*
doctor's office
  l'ambulatorio (m)
dog *il cane*
doll *la bambola*
dolphin *il delfino*
don't *non*

door *la porta*
doorbell *il campanello*
dosage *il dosaggio*
double bed *il letto matrimoniale*
double room *la camera doppia*
do (verb) *fare*
down *giù*
download (verb) *scaricare*
drain *il canale di scolo*
drawer *il cassetto*
drawing *il disegno*
draw (verb) *disegnare*
dress *l'abito (m)*
dressing *la fasciatura*
drink (noun) *la bibita*
drink (verb) *bere*
drinks *le bibite*
drive (verb) *guidare*
driver *l'autista (m)*
driver's license *la patente di guida*
drugstore *la farmacia degli assegni*
dry (day; clothes) *asciutto/a*
dry (wine) *secco*
duck *l'anatra (f)*
duffel bag *la sacca da viaggio*
during *durante*
dust pan *la paletta*
duty-free store *il negozio duty-free*
DVD *il disco DVD*
DVD player *il lettore DVD*

E

each *ciascuno*
each (every) *ogni*
ear *l'orecchio (m)*
early *presto*
earrings *l'orecchino (m)*

earthquake *il terremoto*
east *l'est (m)*
easy *facile*
eat-in *mangiare sul posto*
eating out *mangiare fuori*
eat (verb) *mangiare*
egg *l'uovo (m)*
eggplant *la melanzana (f)*
eight *otto*
elbow *il gomito*
electric razor *il rasoio elettrico*
electrician *l'elettricista (m)*
electricity *l'elettricità (f)*
elevator *l'ascensore (m)*
eleven *undici*
email *l'e-mail (f)*
email address *l'indirizzo e-mail (m)*
embarrassed *imbarazzata*
embassy *l'ambasciata (f)*
emergency *l'emergenza (f)*
emergency exit *l'uscita di emergenza (f)*
emergency room *il pronto soccorso*
emergency services *gli servizi di emergenza*
emigrate (verb) *emigrare*
empty *vuoto/a*
end *la fine*
engaged/busy *occupato/a*
engine *il motore*
English *inglese*
engraving *l'incisione (f)*
enjoy (verb) *divertirsi*
entrance *l'entrata (f)*
entrance ramp *la rampa di accesso*
entrance ticket *il biglietto d'entrata*
envelope *la busta*
epileptic *epilettico/a*
equipment *l'attrezzatura (f)*
espresso *l'espresso (m)*

euro *l'euro (m)*
evening *la sera*
evening dress *l'abito da sera (m)*
evening menu *il menù della cena*
events *le discipline*
every *tutti*
exactly *esattamente*
examine (verb) *esaminare*
exchange rate *il tasso di cambio*
excited *entusiasta*
excursion *l'escursione (f)*
excuse me *mi scusi*
exercise bike *la bicicletta*
exhaust (car) *la marmitta*
exhibition *l'esposizione (f)*
exit *l'uscita (f)*
expensive *caro/a*
expiration date *la data di scadenza*
express service
  il servizio espresso
extension cord *la prolunga*
extra *extra*
eye *l'occhio (m)*
eyebrow *il sopracciglio*
eyelash *il ciglio*
eyeliner *la matita per gli occhi*

F

fabric *il tessuto*
face *il viso*
faint (verb) *svenire*
fairground *il luna park*
fall *l'autunno (m)*
family *la famiglia*
family room *la camera familiare*
family ticket *il biglietto famiglia*
fan *il ventilatore*
far *lontano*
fare *la tariffa*
farm *la fattoria*
farmer *l'agricoltore (m)*
fashion *la moda*
fast *veloce*

fast food *il fast food*
fat *il grasso*
father *il padre*
faucet *il rubinetto*
favorite *preferito/a*
February *febbraio*
female *la donna*
fence *il recinto*
ferry *il traghetto*
festivals *le feste*
fever *la febbre*
field *il campo*
fifty *cinquanta*
fillet *il filetto*
film (camera) *il rullino*
find (verb) *trovare*
fine (legal) *la multa*
finger *il dito*
finish (verb) *finire*
fins *le pinne*
fire *l'incendio (m)*
fire alarm
  l'allarme antincendio (m)
fire engine *l'autopompa (f)*
fire escape *la scala di sicurezza*
fire extinguisher *l'estintore (m)*
firefighter *il pompiere*
fire hydrant *l'idrante (m)*
first *primo/a*
first aid *il pronto soccorso*
first-aid box *la cassetta*
  di pronto soccorso
fish *il pesce*
fishing rod *la canna da pesca*
fish seller *il pescivendolo*
fitting room *lo spogliatoio*
fitness *il fitness*
five *cinque*
fix (verb) *riparare*
flag *la bandierina*
flash gun *il flash*
flash photography *la fotografia*
  con il flash

flashlight *la torcia*
flat *il bemolle*
flight *il volo*
flight attendant *l'assistente di volo (f)*
flight number *il numero del volo*
flip-flop *l'infradito (f)*
float *la tavoletta*
flood *l'inondazione (f)*
floor *il pavimento*
florist *la fioraia/il fioraio*
flowers *i fiori*
flu *l'influenza (f)*
fly (verb) *volare*
fog *la nebbia*
food *il cibo*
foot *il piede*
footpath *il sentiero*
for *per*
foreign currency *la valuta estera*
forest *la foresta*
fork *la forchetta*
fortnight *quindici giorni*
forty *quaranta*
forward *l'attaccante (m)*
fountain *la fontana*
four *quattro*
fracture *la frattura*
fragile *fragile*
frame *la struttura*
free *libero*
free (no charge) *gratis*
free (not occupied) *libero/a*
freeze *la gelata*
French press *la caffettiera*
fresh *fresco/a*
Friday *venerdì*
fried *fritto*
friend *l'amico/a (m/f)*
from *da*
front; in front of *davanti; di fronte a*
front door *il portone*

frost *il gelo*
frozen *congelato/a*
fruit *la frutta*
frying pan *la padella*
fry (verb) *friggere*
fuel gauge *l'indicatore di livello del carburante (m)*
full *pieno/a*
furniture store *il negozio di arredamento*
fuse box *la scatola dei fusibili*

G

gallery (theatre) *la galleria*
game *il gioco*
garage *il garage*
garbage can *la pattumiera*
garden *il giardino*
garlic *l'aglio (m)*
gas *il gas*
gasoline *il carburante*
gas station *la stazione di servizio*
gate *il cancello*
gearshift *la leva del cambio*
get off (verb) *scendere*
gift *il regalo*
gift store *il negozio di articoli da regalo*
gin *il gin*
ginger *lo zenzero*
giraffe *la giraffa*
girl *la ragazza*
girlfriend *la fidanzata*
give (verb) *dare*
glass *il vetro*
glass (drinking) *il bicchiere*
glasses *gli occhiali*
gloss *lucido/a*
gloves *i guanti*
glue *la colla*
go (verb) *andare*
go out (verb) *uscire*

goggles *gli occhialini*
gold *l'oro (m)*
golf *il golf*
golf ball *la palla da golf*
golf club *la mazza*
golf course *il campo da golf*
golf tee *il tee*
good *buono/a*
good afternoon *buon pomeriggio*
good evening *buonasera*
good morning *buongiorno*
good night *buonanotte*
goodbye *arrivederci*
GPS receiver *il navigatore satellitare*
gram *il grammo*
grater *la grattugia*
gray *grigio/a*
graze *l'escoriazione (f)*
Great Britain *la Gran Bretagna*
green *verde*
green tea *il tè verde*
green slopes *le discese per i principianti*
griddle pan *la griglia*
groceries *la spesa*
ground *macinato*
group *il gruppo*
guarantee *la garanzia*
guest *l'ospite (m/f)*
guide (person) *la guida*
guidebook *la guida*
guided tour *la visita guidata*
gym *la palestra*

H

hail *la grandine*
hair *i capelli*
hairdresser's *il parrucchiere*
half *la metà; mezzo/a (adj)*
hand *la mano*
handbag *la borsa*
hand luggage

il bagaglio a mano
handle *la maniglia*
happen (verb) *succedere*
happy *contento/a; felice*
harbor *il porto*
hard *duro/a*
hardware store *la ferramenta*
hat *il cappello*
hatchback *il portellone*
hate (verb) *odiare*
have (verb) *avere*
hayfever *il raffreddore da fieno*
hazard lights *le frecce lampeggianti*
he *egli; lui*
head *la testa*
head rest *il poggiatesta*
headache *il mal di testa*
headlight *i fari*
headphones *le cuffie*
health *la salute*
health insurance *l'assicurazione sanitaria*
hear (verb) *sentire*
heart *il cuore*
heart condition *la patologia cardiaca*
heater *l'impianto di riscaldamento (m)*
heating *il riscaldamento*
heavy *pesante*
heel *il tallone*
height *l'altezza*
hello *ciao; buongiorno*
hello (on phone) *pronto*
help *aiuto*
help (verb) *aiutare*
her (object) *lei; le*
her (possessive) *suo/sua (sing)/sue/suoi (plural)*
herb *l'erba aromatica*
here *qui*

high blood pressure *la pressione arteriosa elevata*

high chair *il seggiolone*

high-speed train *il treno ad alta velocità*

highway *l'autostrada (f)*

hiking *l'escursionismo (m)*

hiking boots *gli scarponi*

hill *la collina*

him *lui: gli*

hip *l'anca (f)*

hockey *l'hockey (m)*

hold (verb) *tenere*

hood *il cappuccio*

hood (car) *il cofano*

horn *il clacson*

horse *il cavallo*

horseback riding *andare a cavallo*

hospital *l'ospedale (m)*

host *il padrone di casa*

hot *caldo/a*

hot (spicy) *piccante*

hot chocolate *la cioccolata calda*

hot drinks *le bevande calde*

hotel *l'albergo (m)*

hour *l'ora (f)*

house *la casa*

hovercraft *l'hovercraft*

how *come?*

how many? *quanti/e?*

how much? *quanto/a?*

humid *umido/a*

hundred *cento*

hurricane *l'uragano (m)*

hurry (verb) *affrettarsi*

husband *il marito*

hydrofoil *l'aliscafo (m)*

I

I (1st person) *io*

ice *il ghiaccio*

ice-skating *il pattinaggio su ghiaccio*

icy *ghiacciato/a*

ID *la carta d'identità*

ill *malato/a*

illness *la malattia*

immigration *l'immigrazione (f)*

in *in*

inbox *la posta in arrivo*

inch *il pollice*

infection *l'infezione (f)*

in-flight meal *il pasto a bordo*

inhaler *l'inalatore (m)*

injection *l'iniezione (f)*

injure (verb) *ferirsi*

injury *la ferita*

insect repellent *il repellente per gli insetti*

inside *all'interno*

instructions *le istruzioni*

insurance *l'assicurazione (f)*

insurance company *l'agenzia assicurativa (f)*

insurance policy *la polizza assicurativa*

intensive care unit *il reparto di terapia intensiva*

interest (verb) *interessare*

interesting *interessante*

internet *l'Internet (m)*

internet café *l'internet cafè*

interpreter *l'interprete (m/f)*

into *dentro*

inventory *l'inventario (m)*

iPod *l'iPod (m)*

iron *il ferro da stiro*

ironing board *l'asse a stiro (f)*

island *l'isola (f)*

it *esso/a; lo/la; gli/le*

Italian *italiano/a*
Italy *l'Italia (f)*

J

jacket *la giacca*
jam *la marmellata*
January *gennaio*
jar *il barattolo*
jaw *la mascella*
jazz club *il jazz club*
jeans *i jeans*
jellyfish *la medusa*
jet ski *la moto d'acqua*
jet skiing *l'acquascooter*
jeweler *il gioielliere*
jewelry *la gioielleria*
jogging *il footing*
juice *il succo*
July *luglio*
June *giugno*

K

kayak *il kayak*
keep straight *andare dritto*
ketchup *il ketchup*
kettle *il bollitore*
key *la chiave*
keyboard *la tastiera*
kilo *il chilo*
kilogram *il chilogrammo*
kilometer *il chilometro*
kitchen *la cucina*
knee *il ginocchio*
knife *il coltello*
knock down (verb) *colpire*
know (a fact) *sapere*
know (people) *conoscere*

L

labels *le etichette*

lake *il lago*
lamb *l'agnello (m)*
laptop *il computer portatile*
large *grande*
last *ultimo/a*
last week *la settimana scorsa*
late *tardi; in ritardo*
laugh (verb) *ridere*
laundromat *la lavanderia*
lawyer *l'avvocato (m)*
leak *la perdita*
learn (verb) *imparare*
leave (verb) *lasciare; partire*
left *sinistra*
left luggage *il deposito bagagli*
leg *la gamba*
leisure *il tempo libero*
leisure activities *le attività del tempo libero*
lemon *il limone*
lemon grass *la citronella*
lemonade *la limonata*
length *la lunghezza*
lens *la lente*
less *meno*
letter carrier *il postino*
lettuce *la lattuga*
library *la biblioteca*
lid *il coperchio*
life jacket *il giubbotto di salvataggio*
lifeguard *il bagnino*
life ring *il salvagente*
lift pass *il pass per lo ski-lift*
light *leggero/a*
light (noun) *la luce*
light (verb) *accendere*
light bulb *la lampadina*
lighter *l'accendino (m)*
lighthouse *il faro*
lights switch *l'interruttore per le luci*
like (verb) *piacere*

lime *il tiglio*
line *la linea*
liquid *liquido*
list *la lista*
listen (verb) *ascoltare*
liter *il litro*
little *poco; piccolo*
living room *il salotto*
load (verb) *caricare*
loan *il prestito*
local *locale*
lock *il lucchetto*
lockers *gli armadietti*
lock (verb) *chiudere a chiave*
log on (verb) *connettersi*
log out (verb) *disconnettersi*
long *lungo*
look (verb) *guardare*
lose (verb) *perdere*
lost property *l'ufficio
 oggetti smarriti (m)*
lounge chair *il lettino sdraio*
love *a zero*
love (verb) *amare*
low *basso/a*
luggage *il bagaglio*
luggage rack *il portabagagli*
lunch *il pranzo*
lunch menu *il menù del pranzo*

M

magazine *la rivista*
mail *la posta*
mail (verb) *spedire la posta*
mailbox *la cassetta delle lettere*
main course *il piatto principale*
make (verb) *fare*
makeup *il trucco*
mallet *il maglio*
man *l'uomo (m)*
manager *il capo*
mango *il mango*
manicure *la manicure*

manual *il manuale*
manuscript *il manoscritto*
many *molti/e*
map *la mappa; la cartina*
March *marzo*
marina *il porticciolo*
market *il mercato*
marmalade *la marmellata
 di agrumi*
married *sposato/a*
mascara *il mascara*
massage *il massaggio*
match (light) *il fiammifero*
match (sport) *la partita*
matte *opaco/a*
mattress *il materasso*
May *maggio*
maybe *forse*
mayonnaise *la maionese*
measure *la misura*
meat *la carne*
meatballs *le polpette*
mechanic *il meccanico*
medicine *la medicina*
medium *mezzo*
memory card *la scheda
 di memoria*
memory stick *la chiavetta USB*
mend (verb) *riparare*
menu *il menù*
message *il messaggio*
messages *i messaggi*
metal *il metallo*
meter *il metro*
microwave *il forno a microonde*
middle *mezzo*
midnight *mezzanotte*
migraine *l'emicrania (f)*
mile *il miglio*
milk *il latte*
mineral water *l'acqua
 minerale (f)*
mini bar *il mini bar*

mint *la menta*
minute *il minuto*
mirror *lo specchio*
mistake *l'errore (m)*
misty *nebbioso/a*
mixed *misto/a*
mixing bowl *l'insalatiera (f)*
mole (medical) *il neo*
Monday *lunedì*
money *il denaro; i soldi*
monkey *la scimmia*
month *il mese*
monument *il monumento*
mooring *l'ormeggio (m)*
more *più*
morning *il mattino*
mosquito *la zanzara*
mosquito net *la zanzariera*
mother *la madre*
motorcycle *la motocicletta*
mountain *la montagna*
mountain bike
  la mountain bike
mouse *il topo*
mouse (computer) *il mouse*
mouth *la bocca*
mouthwash *il collutorio*
move *la mossa*
movie *il film*
movie theater *il cinema*
mozzarella *la mozzarella*
much *molto*
muffin *il muffin*
mug *la tazza*
muscles *i muscoli*
museum *il museo*
mushroom *il fungo*
music *la musica*
musician *il musicista*
mustard *la senape*
must (verb) *dovere*
my *mio/mia/mie/miei*
myself *mi; me stesso/a*

N

nail *l'unghia (f)*
nail clippers *i tagliaunghie*
nail scissors *le forbicine*
  per le unghie
name *il nome*
napkin *il tovagliolo*
narrow *stretto*
national park *il parco nazionale*
natural *naturale*
nausea *la nausea*
navigate (verb) *navigare*
neck *il collo*
necklace *la collana*
need (verb) *aver bisogno*
nervous *nervoso/a*
net *la rete*
network *la rete*
never *mai*
new *nuovo/a*
news *il telegiornale*
newspaper *il giornale*
newsstand *l'edicola (f)*
next *prossimo/a*
next to *vicino a*
next week *la settimana prossima*
nice *bello/a; piacevole*
night *la notte*
nightclub *la discoteca*
nine *nove*
no *no*
no entry *ingresso vietato*
noisy *rumoroso/a*
noon *mezzogiorno*
normal *normale*
north *il nord*
nose *il naso*
nosebleed *il sangue dal naso*
not *non*
notebook *il blocco*
November *novembre*
now *adesso*
number *il numero*

number plate *il numero di targa*
nurse *l'infermiere (m)*
nuts *le noccioline*

O

oar *il timone*
oats *l'avena (f)*
occupations *i mestieri*
occupied *occupato*
ocean *l'oceano (m)*
October *ottobre*
octopus *la piovra; il polpo*
of *di*
off *spento/a*
office *l'ufficio (m)*
often *spesso*
oil *l'olio (m)*
ointment *la pomata*
OK *d'accordo*
old *vecchio*
olive oil *l'olio d'oliva (m)*
olives *le olive*
omelet *la frittata*
on *su*
one *uno/a*
onion *la cipolla*
on (light) *acceso/a*
one-way ticket *il biglietto*
online *online*
only *solamente*
onto *sopra*
open *aperto/a*
open (verb) *aprire*
opening hours
  l'orario di apertura (m)
opening times
  l'orario di apertura (m)
opera *l'opera (f)*
opera house *il teatro dell'opera*
operation
  l'intervento chirurgico (m)
opposite *davanti; di fronte*

or *o*
orange (color) *arancione*
orange juice *il succo d'arancia*
order *l'ordine (m)*
order (verb) *ordinare*
other *altro/a*
our *nostro/nostri/nostra/nostre*
outside *fuori*
oven *il forno*
oven mitts *i guanti da forno*
over *su; sopra*
overdraft *lo scoperto*
overhead bin
  il compartimento portabagagli
overnight *tutta la notte*
owe (verb) *essere in debito*

P

pack (verb) *fare le valigie*
package *il pacco*
pack of cards *il mazzo di carte*
packet *il pacchetto*
pads *le ginocchiere*
pajamas *il pigiama*
pail *il secchio*
pain *il dolore*
painkiller *l'antidolorifico (m)*
painting *il dipinto*
pair *la coppia*
pan *il piatto*
pan fried *fritto in padella*
pants *i pantaloni*
panty hose *il collant*
paper *la carta*
papers (ID) *i documenti*
parents *i genitori*
park *il parco*
park (verb) *parcheggiare*
parka *il giaccone (m)*
parking *il parcheggio*
parking lot *il parcheggio*
parking meter *il parchimetro*
parmesan *il parmigiano*

parsley *il prezzemolo*
partner *il compagno/la compagna*
pass *il passaggio*
pass (verb) *sorpassare*
passenger *la passeggera*
passport *il passaporto*
passport control
  il controllo passaporti
pasta *la pasta*
pastry *le paste*
path *il viottolo*
patient *la paziente*
pause *la pausa*
pay (verb) *pagare*
pay in (verb) *effettuare un deposito*
payment *il pagamento*
payphone *il telefono pubblico*
peanut *l'arachide (f)*
peanut butter *il burro di arachidi*
pear *la pera*
pedestrian crossing
  l'attraversamento pedonale (m)
pedicure *la pedicure*
peel (verb) *sbucciare*
peeler *lo sbucciatore*
pen *la penna*
pencil *la matita*
people *la gente; le persone*
pepper *il pepe*
perfume *il profumo*
perhaps *forse*
personal CD player *il lettore CD*
pet *l'animale domestico (m)*
pharmacist *il/la farmacista*
pharmacy *la farmacia*
phone *il telefono*
phone call *la telefonata*
phone card *la carta telefonica*
photo album *l'album delle
  fotografie (m)*
photo frame *la cornice*
photograph(y) *la fotografia*
pianist *il/la pianista*

picnic *il picnic*
picnic basket *il cestino da picnic*
pie *il pasticcio*
piece *il pezzo*
pilates *pilates*
pill *la compressa*
pillow *il cuscino*
pilot *il/la pilota*
PIN *il PIN*
pink *rosa*
pint *la pinta*
pitch *il campo di cricket*
pitch a tent (verb)
  piantare una tenda
pitcher *la brocca*
pizza *la pizza*
place *il luogo*
plane *la pialla*
planet *il pianeta*
plants *le piante*
plate *il piatto*
platform *il binario*
play *l'opera teatrale (f)*
play (games) (verb) *giocare*
playground *l'area giochi (f)*
please *per favore*
plug *la spina*
plum *la prugna*
plumber *l'idraulico (m)*
pocket *la tasca*
point *il punto*
poles (ski) *le racchette da sci*
police *la polizia*
police car *la volante*
police officer *il poliziotto (m)/la
  poliziotta*
police station *il commissariato*
policy *la polizza*
pool *la piscina*
pork *il maiale*
porridge *la pappa d'avena*
porter *il facchino*
portion *la porzione*

possible *possibile*
postage *l'affrancatura (f)*
postcard *la cartolina*
post office *l'ufficio postale (m)*
potato *la patata*
potato chips *le patatine*
poultry *il pollame*
pound *la libbra*
pour (verb) *versare*
powder *la polvere*
power *l'elettricità (f)*
power outage *l'interruzione di corrente (f)*
prefer (verb) *preferire*
pregnancy test *il test di gravidanza*
pregnant *incinta*
prescription *la ricetta medica*
present *il regalo*
press *la stampa*
price *il prezzo*
price list *il listino*
print *la fotografia (sviluppata)*
print (photo) *la stampa*
print (verb) *stampare*
produce seller *il fruttivendolo*
program *il programma*
proud *fiero/a*
prove (verb) *lievitare*
province *la provincia*
public holiday *il giorno festivo*
pump (bicycle) *la pompa*
puncture *la gomma a terra*
purple *viola*
push *spingere*
put (verb) *mettere*

Q, R

quarter *il quarto*
quick *rapido/a; veloce*
quite *abbastanza*
rabbit *il coniglio*
race *la gara*

racecourse *l'ippodromo (m)*
rack *la rastrelliera*
radiator *il radiatore*
radio *la radio*
rail *la rotaia*
railroad *la ferrovia*
rain boots *le galosce*
rain forest *la foresta pluviale*
raining *piovendo*
rape *la violenza carnale*
rarely *raramente*
rash *l'eruzione (f)*
raspberry *il lampone*
rat *il ratto*
raw *crudo/a*
razor *il rasoio*
read (verb) *leggere*
ready *pronto/a*
real estate office *l'agenzia immobiliare (f)*
really *veramente*
receipt *la ricevuta*
receive (verb) *ricevere*
reception *la ricezione*
receptionist *l'addetto/a alla ricezione (m/f)*
reclaim tag *la ricevuta dei bagagli*
recommend (verb) *consigliare*
record *il primato*
record store *il negozio di dischi*
recycling bin *il contenitore di riciclaggio*
red *rosso/a*
reduction *la riduzione*
refrigerator *il frigorifero*
region *la regione*
relatives *i parenti*
release (verb) *rilasciare*
remote control *il telecomando*
rent (verb) *affittare; noleggiare*
repair (verb) *riparare*
report (verb) *denunciare*
research *la ricerca*

reservation *la prenotazione*
reserve (verb) *prenotare; riservare*
rest *la pausa*
restroom *il bagno*
restaurant *il ristorante*
resuscitation *la rianimazione*
retired *in pensione*
return *il ritorno*
return ticket *il biglietto di andata e ritorno*
reverse (verb) *fare marcia indietro*
rewind *il riavvolgimento*
rib *la costola*
rice *il riso*
rides *le giostre*
right (direction) *destra*
ring *l'anello (m)*
rinse (verb) *sciacquare*
ripe *maturo/a*
river *il fiume*
road *la strada*
roads *le strade*
road signs *segnali stradali (m pl)*
roadwork *i lavori stradali*
roast *l'arrosto (m)*
rob (verb) *derubare*
robbery *il furto*
robe *la toga*
rock climbing *l'alpinismo in parete (m)*
rocks *le rocce*
roll (film) *il rullino*
romance *il film d'amore*
roof *il tetto*
roofrack *il bagagliaio*
room *la stanza; la camera*
room key *la chiave della camera*
root *la radice*
rope *la corda*
rough *il rough*
round *rotondo/a*
router *router (f)*
row *la fila*

rowing machine *il vogatore*
ruby *il rubino*
rug *il tappeto*
run *il giro*
rush *il giunco*

S

sad *triste*
safari park *il parco safari*
safe *sicuro/a*
sailing *la vela*
sailing boat *la barca a vela*
salad *l'insalata (f)*
salami *il salame*
sales assistant *commesso/a*
salmon *il salmone*
saloon car *la berlina*
salt *il sale*
salted *salato/a*
same *stesso/a*
sand *la sabbia*
sandals *i sandali*
sandwich *il tramezzino*
sanitary napkin *l'assorbente (m)*
satellite navigation *la navigazione via satellite*
satellite TV *la TV satellitare*
Saturday *sabato*
sauce *la salsa*
saucepan *la pentola*
saucer *il piattino*
sauna *la sauna*
sausage *il wurstel*
sauté (verb) *rosolare*
save (verb) *parare*
savings account *il conto di risparmio*
savory *salato/a*
say (verb) *dire*
scale *la bilancia*
scan *l'ecografia (f)*
scared *spaventato/a*
scarf *la sciarpa*

school *la scuola*
scissors *le forbici*
scoop *la pallina*
score *lo spartito*
scuba diving *il nuoto subacqueo*
sea *il mare*
seafood *i frutti di mare*
search (verb) *cercare*
season *la stagione*
seasons *le stagioni*
seat *il posto; la sedia*
second *secondo/a*
second floor *il primo piano*
security *la sicurezza*
seedless *senza semi*
seeds *i semi*
see (verb) *vedere*
sell (verb) *vendere*
sell-by date *la data di scadenza*
send (verb) *inviare;
mandare; spedire*
send off *l'espulsione (f)*
senior citizen *anziano/a*
sensitive *sensibile*
sentence *la sentenza*
separately *separatamente*
September *settembre*
serious *grave; serio/a*
serve *il servizio*
serve (verb) *servire*
server *cameriere/a*
services *i servizi*
set *la scenografia*
seven *sette*
sew (verb) *cucire*
shampoo *lo shampoo*
shark *lo squalo*
sharp *il diesis*
shaving foam *la schiuma da barba*
she *ella; lei*
sheet *il lenzuolo*
shelf *lo scaffale*
shelves *la mensola*

sherbet *il sorbetto*
shirt *la camicia*
shock *lo shock*
shoe *la scarpa*
shoes *le scarpe*
shoe store *il negozio di calzature*
shopping *fare la spesa*
shopping mall
il centro commerciale
short *corto/a*
shorts *i calzoncini*
shoulder *la spalla*
shout (verb) *gridare*
shower *la doccia*
shower gel *il docciaschiuma*
shy *timida*
sick *malato/a*
side *il lato*
side-by-side refrigerator *il
frigorifero congelatore*
side effect *l'effetto
indesiderato (m)*
side order *il contorno*
side plate *il piattino*
sidewalk *il marciapiede*
sightseeing *il giro turistico*
sign *l'insegna (f)*
signal *il segnale*
signature *la firma*
signpost *il cartello*
silk *la seta*
silver *l'argento (m)*
singer *cantante (m/f)*
single bed *il letto singolo*
single room *la camera singola
di sola andata*
sink *il lavandino*
siren *la sirena*
sister *la sorella*
six *sei*
size *la taglia*
skate *il pattino*
sketch *lo schizzo*

ski *lo sci*
ski boots *gli scarponi da sci*
ski slope *la pista da sci*
skiing *lo sci*
skin *la pelle*
skirt *la gonna*
skis *gli sci*
sleeper berth *la cuccetta*
sleeping *dormire*
sleeping bag *il sacco a pelo*
sleeping pill *il sonnifero*
slice *la fetta*
slickers *gli indumenti impermeabili*
slide *lo scivolo*
slip *la sottoveste*
slippers *le pantofole*
sliproad *la bretella*
slope *la pendenza*
slow *lento/a*
slow down *rallentare*
small *piccolo/a*
smartphone *lo smartphone*
smash *la schiacciata*
smile *il sorriso*
smoke *il fumo*
smoke (verb) *fumare*
smoke alarm *il rivelatore di fumo*
smoking area *area fumatori*
snack *lo spuntino*
snack bar *il dolciume*
snake *il serpente*
sneakers
  le scarpe da ginnastica
sneeze *lo starnuto*
sneeze (verb) *starnutire*
snore (verb) *russare*
snorkel *il boccaglio*
snow *la neve*
snow (verb) *nevicare*
snowboard *lo snowboard*
snowboarding *lo snowboard*
so *così*
soak (verb) *mettere a bagno*

soap *il sapone*
soccer (ball) *il pallone*
soccer (game) *il calcio*
socks *i calzini*
soda water *la soda*
sofa *il divano*
sofa bed *il divano letto*
soft *morbido/a*
soft drinks *le bibite*
soil *il terreno*
some *alcuni/e*
somebody *qualcuno/a*
something *qualcosa*
sometimes *qualche volta*
son *il figlio*
song *la canzone*
soon *presto*
sore *infiammato/a*
sorry *scusi*
soup *la minestra*
sour *agro/a*
south *il sud*
souvenir *il souvenir*
spare tire *la ruota di scorta*
spatula *la spatola*
speak (verb) *parlare*
speaker *l'oratore/ l'oratrice*
speciality *la specialità*
specials *le specialità*
speed limit *il limite di velocità*
speedometer *il tachimetro*
spices *le spezie*
spider *il ragno*
spinach *gli spinaci*
spine *la spina dorsale*
splint *la stecca*
splinter *la scheggia*
spoke *il raggio*
sponge *la spugna*
spoon *il cucchiaio*
sport *lo sport*
sports *gli articoli sportivi*
sports center *il centro sportivo*

sprain *la distorsione*
spray *lo spray*
spring *la primavera*
square *il quadrato*
square (in town) *la piazza*
squash (game) *lo squash*
staff *il personale*
stage *il palcoscenico*
staircase *la scala*
stairs *le scale*
stalls *la platea*
stamp *il francobollo*
stand *il sostegno*
start (verb) *cominciare*
statement *la dichiarazione*
station *la stazione*
statue *la statua*
stay *il soggiorno*
steak *la bistecca*
steamed *al vapore*
step machine *la step machine*
stew *il minestrone*
stick *la mazza*
sting *il pungiglione*
stir-fry *la frittura*
stir (verb) *rimestare*
stolen *rubato/a*
stomach *lo stomaco*
stomach ache *il mal di stomaco*
stone *la pietra preziosa*
stop (verb) *fermare*
stop *lo stop*
stop (bus) *la fermata*
store *il negozio*
stormy *tempestoso/a*
straight *dritto*
strap *la spallina*
strawberry *la fragola*
street *la strada; la via*
street map *la cartina; la mappa*
street sign *il segnale stradale*
stress *lo stress*
string *la corda*

strong *forte*
student
 lo studente/ la studentessa
student card *la carta studenti*
study *lo studio*
stuffed animal *il peluche*
suburb *la periferia*
subway
 la metropolitana
subway map
 la mappa della metropolitana
suit *il completo*
suitcase *la valigia*
summer *l'estate (f)*
sun *il sole*
sunbathe (verb) *prendere il sole*
sunbed *il lettino solare*
sunblock *la crema schermo totale*
sunburn *la bruciatura*
Sunday *domenica*
sunflower oil *l'olio di*
 semi di girasole
sunglasses *gli occhiali da sole*
sunhat *il cappello da sole*
sunny *assolato/a*
sunrise *il sorgere del sole*
sunscreen *il filtro solare*
sunset *il tramonto*
sunshine *la luce del sole*
suntan lotion *la lozione solare*
supermarket *il supermercato*
support *il supporto*
suppositories *le supposte*
surf *la cresta dell'onda*
surf (verb) *fare surf*
surfboard *la tavola da surf*
surgeon *il/la chirurgo*
surgery *l'ambulatorio (m)*
surprised *sorpreso/a*
sweater *il maglione*
sweatshirt *la felpa*
sweep (verb) *spazzare*
sweet *dolce*

sweet potato *la patata dolce*
swim (verb) *nuotare*
swimming *il nuoto*
swimming pool *la piscina*
swimsuit *il costume*
swing *l'altalena (f)*
switch *l'interruttore (m)*

T

table *il tavolo*
tablet *la compressa*
tailor *il sarto/la sarta*
take (verb) *prendere*
take off (verb) *decollare*
tall *alto/a*
tampon *il tampone*
tan *l'abbronzatura (f)*
tank *il serbatoio*
tax *l'imposta (f)*
taxi *il taxi*
taxi driver *il/la tassista*
taxi stand *il posteggio dei taxi*
tea *il tè*
teabag *la bustina di tè*
team *la squadra*
teapot *la teiera*
teaspoon *il cucchiaino*
teeth *i denti*
telephone *il telefono*
telephone (verb) *telefonare*
telephone box *la cabina del telefono*
television (set) *il televisore*
tell (verb) *dire*
temperature *la temperatura*
ten *dieci*
tennis *il tennis*
tennis ball *la palla da tennis*
tennis court *il campo da tennis*
tennis racket *la racchetta da tennis*
tent *la tenda*
tent peg *il picchetto*

terminal *il terminal*
test *l'analisi (f)*
text (SMS) *il messaggio (SMS)*
than *di*
thank you *grazie*
that *quello/a*
the *il/lo/la/i/gli/le*
theater *il teatro*
their *loro*
then *poi; allora*
there *là*
there is/are *c'è/ci sono*
thermometer *il termometro*
thermostat *termostato (m)*
thick *spesso/a*
thief *ladro (m)*
thin *sottile*
think (verb) *pensare*
third floor *il secondo piano*
thirty *trenta*
this *questo/a*
thousand *mille*
three *tre*
throat *la gola*
throat lozenge *la pasticca per la gola*
through *attraverso*
throw *la proiezione*
thumb *il pollice*
Thursday *giovedì*
ticket *il biglietto*
ticket gates *la barriera*
ticket inspector *il controllore*
ticket office *la biglietteria*
tie *la cravatta*
tight *stretto/a*
tile *la pedina*
time *il tempo*
timetable *l'orario (m)*
tip *la punta*
tire *il pneumatico*
tire pressure *la pressione degli pneumatici*

tissue il fazzolettino
toast il pane tostato
toaster il tostapane
tobacco il tabacco
tobacconist il tabaccaio (m)
today oggi
toe il dito del piede
toiletries gli articoli da toeletta
toilet paper la carta igienica
toll il pedaggio
tomato il pomodoro
tomato sauce il ketchup
tomorrow domani
tongue la lingua
tonight stasera
too (excessively) troppo/a
tooth il dente
toothache il mal di denti
toothbrush lo spazzolino da denti
toothpaste il dentifricio
tour il giro
tour bus il pullman turistico
tour guide la guida turistica
tourist il/la turista (m/f)
tourist attraction il luogo
  d'interesse turistico
tourist information l'ufficio
  informazioni turistiche (m)
tourist information office
  l'ufficio del turismo (m)
towards verso
towel l'asciugamano (m)
towels gli asciugamani
town la città
town center il centro della città
town hall il municipio
tow (verb) rimorchiare
toy il giocattolo
track il binario
traffic il traffico
traffic circle la rotatoria
traffic jam l'ingorgo
traffic lights il semaforo

train il treno
train station
  la stazione ferroviaria
tram il tram
transportation i trasporti
trash il cestino
trash can la pattumiera
travel agent l'agente
  di viaggio (m)
traveler's check
  il travellers check
travel-sickness pills
  le pasticche antinausea
tray il vassoio
tree l'albero (m)
trekking
  l'escursione a cavallo (f)
trip la gita
tripod il treppiede
trout la trota
trunk (car) il bagagliaio
try la meta
try (verb) provare
T-shirt la t-shirt
tub la vaschetta
tube il tubetto
Tuesday martedì
tumble dryer
  l'asciuga-biancheria (f)
tuna il tonno
turn off (verb) spegnere
turn (verb) girare; voltare
tweezers la pinzetta
twenty venti
twin room
  la camera a due letti
two due

U

ugly brutto/a
umbrella l'ombrello (m)
uncle lo zio
under sotto

underpass *il sottopassaggio*
undershirt *la canottiera*
understand (verb)
  capire; comprendere
underwear *la biancheria intima*
uniform *l'uniforme (f)*
United States *gli Stati Uniti*
university *l'università (f)*
unleaded *senza piombo*
until *fino a*
up *su*
upset *adirato/a*
urgent *urgente*
us *noi*
useful *utile*
use (verb) *usare*
usual *solito/a*
usually *generalmente*

V

vacancy (room) *la stanza libera*
vacation *la vacanza*
vacuum flask *il thermos*
validate (verb) *vidimare*
valuables *gli oggetti di valore*
vegetables *la verdura*
vegetarian *vegetariano/a*
veggie burger *l'hamburger*
  vegetariano (m)
venetian blind
  la tenda veneziana
very *molto*
veterinarian *il veterinario/la*
  veterinaria
video game *il videogioco*
view *la vista*
village *il villaggio*
vinegar *l'aceto (m)*
vineyard *il vigneto*
virus *il virus*
visa *il visto*
vision *la vista*
visiting hours

  l'orario delle visite (m)
visitor *il visitatore*
vitamins *le vitamine*
voice message
  il messaggio vocale
volume *il volume*
vomit (verb) *vomitare*

W

wait (verb) *aspettare*
waiting room *la sala d'attesa*
waitress *la cameriera*
wake up (verb) *svegliarsi*
wake-up call *la sveglia telefonica*
walk *la passeggiata*
wall *il muro*
wallet *il portafoglio*
want (verb) *volere*
ward *la corsia*
warm *caldo/a*
washing machine *la lavatrice*
wash (verb) *lavare*
wasp *la vespa*
watch *l'orologio da polso*
watch (verb) *guardare*
water *l'acqua (f)*
water bottle *la borraccia*
waterfall *la cascata*
watermelon *l'anguria*
water-skiing *lo sci d'acqua*
watersports *gli sport acquatici*
water valve *il rubinetto di arresto*
water wings *il bracciolo*
wave *l'onda (f)*
wax *la depilazione*
we *noi*
weak *debole*
weather *il tempo*
website *il sito web*
wedding *il matrimonio*
Wednesday *mercoledì*
week *la settimana*
weekend *il fine settimana*

weigh (verb) *pesare*
weight *il peso*
welcome *benvenuto/a*
well *bene*
west *l'ovest (m)*
wet *bagnato/a*
wet wipe
  la salvietta umidificata
wetsuit *la tuta subacquea*
whale *la balena*
what? *cosa?*
wheat *il grano*
wheel *la ruota*
wheelchair *la sedia a rotelle*
wheelchair access *l'accesso per i disabili (m)*
wheelchair ramp
  la rampa per i disabili
when? *quando?*
where? *dove?*
which? *quale?*
whisk *la frusta (f)*
whiskey *il whisky*
white *bianco/a*
who? *chi?*
whole *intero*
whole-wheat bread *il pane integrale*
why? *perché?*
wide *largo/a*
widescreen TV *il televisore a schermo panoramico*
width *la larghezza*
Wi-Fi *Wifi*
wife *la moglie*
win (verb) *vincere*
wind *il vento*
window *la finestra*
window seat *il posto vicino al finestrino*
windshield *la parabrezza*
windshield wiper
  il tergicristallo

windsurf board *la tavola da surf*
windy *ventoso/a*
wine *il vino*
wine glass *il calice da vino*
wine list *la lista dei vini*
winter *l'inverno (m)*
winter sports *gli sport invernali*
wipe (verb) *pulire*
wiper blades *le spazzole del tergicristallo*
with *con*
withdraw (money) (verb)
  prelevare
withdrawal *il prelievo*
without *senza*
witness *il/la testimone (m/f)*
woman *la donna*
wood *il bosco*
wool *la lana*
work *il lavoro*
work (machine) *funzionare*
work (verb) *lavorare*
worried *preoccupato/a*
worse *peggiore*
wrap (a gift) *incartare*
wrapping paper
  la carta da regalo
wrist *il polso*
wrist watch *l'orologio da polso*
write (verb) *scrivere*
wrong *sbagliato/a*

X, Y, Z

X-ray *la radiografia*
yacht *lo yacht*
year *l'anno (m)*
yellow *giallo/a*
yes *sì*
yesterday *ieri*
yoga *lo yoga*
yogurt *lo yogurt*
you *Lei; tu (singular); voi (plural)*
young *giovane*

zero *zero*
zipper *la chiusura lampo*
zone *la zona*
zoo *lo zoo*
zucchini *la zucchina*

DICTIONARY ITALIAN–ENGLISH

The gender of Italian nouns is shown by the abbreviations **(m)** for masculine and **(f)** for feminine. Plural nouns are followed by the abbreviations **(m pl)** or **(f pl)**. Adjectives vary according to the gender and number of the word they describe. Here the masculine singular form (usually "o") is shown, followed by the alternative feminine ending (usually "a").

A

a *at*
a destra (f) *right*
a sinistra *left*
abbastanza *quite*
abbigliamento (m) *clothing*
abbronzatura (f) *tan*
abiti (m pl) *clothes*
abito (m) *dress*
abito da sera (m)
  evening dress
accamparsi *to camp*
accappatoio (m)
  bath robe
accendere *to light*
accendino (m) *lighter*
acceso *on (light)*
accesso per i disabili (m)
  wheelchair access
aceto (m) *vinegar*
acqua (f) *water*
acqua minerale (m)
  mineral water
acquascooter (m)
  jet skiing
adattatore (m) *adapter*
addebitare *to charge*
addebito diretto (m)
  automatic payment
addetta alla ricezione (f)
  receptionist
adesso *now*

adirato *upset*
adulto (m) *adult*
aerobica (f) *aerobics*
aeroplano (m) *airplane*
aeroporto (m) *airport*
affittare *to rent*
affrancatura (f) *postage*
affrettarsi *to hurry*
agenda (f) *day planner*
agente di viaggio (m)
  travel agent
agenzia assicurativa (f)
  insurance company
agenzia immobiliare (f)
  real estate office
aglio (m) *garlic*
agnello (m) *lamb*
agosto *August*
agricoltore (m) *farmer*
agro *sour*
agrumi (m pl) *citrus fruit*
airbag (m) *airbag*
aiutare *to help*
aiuto (m) *help*
al vapore *steamed*
albergo (m) *hotel*
albero (m) *tree*
albicocca (f) *apricot*
album delle fotografie (m)
  photo album
alcuni/e *some*
aliscafo (m) *hydrofoil*

allarme antincendio (m)
fire alarm
allegato (m) *attachment*
allergia (f) *allergy*
allergico/a *allergic*
all'interno *inside*
alloggio (m) *accommodation*
allora *then*
alpinismo in parete (m)
rock climbing
altalena (f) *swing*
altezza (f) *height*
alto *tall*
altro/a *other;*
un altro/un'altra *another*
amaro *bitter*
ambasciata (f) *embassy*
ambulanza (f) *ambulance*
ambulatorio (m)
doctor's office
amico/a (m/f) *friend*
analisi (f) *test*
analisi del sangue (f pl)
blood test
anatra (f) *duck*
anche *too (also)*
ancora *again*
andare *to go*
andare a cavallo *horseback riding*
andare dritto *to go straight*
andare in bici *to cycle*
andare in discoteca
to go clubbing
anello (m) *ring*
anguria (f) *watermelon*
animale domestico (m) *pet*
animali (m pl) *animals*
anno (m) *year*
annoiato *bored*
antibiotici (m pl) *antibiotics*
antidolorifico (m) *painkiller*
antipasto (m) *appetizer*
anziano/a (m/f)

senior citizen
ape (f) *bee*
aperto/a *open*
appartamento (m)
apartment
appendiabiti (m)
coat hanger
applaudire *to applaud*
applicazione (f)
application
appuntamento (m)
appointment
apribottiglie (m)
bottle/can opener
aprile *April*
aprire *to open*
arachide (f) *peanut*
arancione *orange (color)*
architetto (m) *architect*
architettura (f) *architecture*
arco (m) *arc*
arco plantare (m) *arch*
area fumatori (f)
smoking area
area giochi (f) *playground*
argento (m) *silver*
aria condizionata (f) *air-conditioning*
armadietti (m pl) *lockers*
armadio (m) *closet*
arrabbiata *angry*
arrangiamenti (m pl)
arrangements
arrivare *to arrive*
arrivederci *goodbye*
arrivi (m pl) *arrivals hall*
arrosto (m) *roast*
arte (f) *art*
articoli da toeletta
(m pl) *toiletries*
articoli sportivi
(m pl) *sports*
artista (m/f) *artist*

artrite (f) *arthritis*
ascensore (m) *elevator*
asciuga-biancheria (f)
 tumble dryer
asciugacapelli (m)
 blow-dryer
asciugamani (m pl)
 towels
asciugamano (m) *towel*
asciugamano grande (m)
 bath towel
asciugare con il fon
 to blow dry
asciutto *dry (day; clothes)*
ascoltare *to listen*
asma (f) *asthma*
aspettare *to wait*
aspetto (m) *appearance*
asse da stiro (f)
 ironing board
assegno (m) *check*
assicurazione (f) *insurance*
assicurazione sanitaria (f)
 health insurance
assistente (m/f) *assistant*
assistente di volo (m/f)
 air stewardess
assolato/a *sunny*
assorbente (m)
 sanitary napkin
atleta (m) *athlete*
atrio (m) *concourse*
attaccante (m) *forward*
attacco (m) *attack*
attenzione (f) *caution*
attività (f pl) *activites*
attore (m) *actor*
attorno *around*
attraversamento pedonale (m)
 pedestrian crossing
attraverso *through*
attrezzatura (f) *equipment*
attrice (f) *actress*

audio guida (f) *audio guide*
Australia (f) *Australia*
autista (m/f) *driver*
autobus (m) *bus*
autolavaggio (m)
 car wash
automatico *automatic*
automobile (f) *car*
autonoleggio (m)
 car rental
autopompa (f) *fire engine*
autostrada (f) *highway*
autunno (m) *fall*
avena (f) *oats*
aver bisogno *to need*
avere *to have*
avocado (m) *avocado*
avvocato (m) *lawyer*

B

bacca (f) *berry*
badminton (m) *badminton*
bagaglio (m) *luggage*
bagagliaio (m) *trunk*
 (car); roofrack
bagaglio a mano (m)
 hand luggage
bagaglio consentito (m)
 baggage allowance
bagel (m) *bagel*
bagnato/a *wet*
bagnino (m) *lifeguard*
bagno (m) *bath;*
 bathroom; restroom
bagnoschiuma (m)
 bubblebath
balcone (m) *balcony*
balena (f) *whale*
ballare *dancing*
balsamo (m) *conditioner*
bambini (m) *children*
bambino/a (m/f) *child*
bambola (f) *doll*

banana (f) *banana*
banca (f) *bank*
banco accettazione (m) *check-in desk*
bancomat (m) *ATM*
bandierina (f) *flag*
bar (m) *bar; café*
barattolo (m) *jar*
barbabietola (f) *beet*
barbecue (m) *barbecue*
barbiere (m) *barber*
barca (f) *boat*
barca a vela (f) *sailing boat*
barista (m) *bartender*
barriera (f) *ticket gates*
barriera corallina (f) *coral reef*
baseball (m) *baseball*
basilico (m) *basil*
basso *low*
batteria (f) *battery*
bello/a *beautiful; nice*
bemolle (m) *flat*
benda (f) *bandage*
bene *alright; well*
benvenuto *welcome*
bere *to drink*
berlina (f) *saloon car*
bevande alcoliche (f pl) *alcoholic drinks*
bevande calde (f pl) *hot drinks*
biancheria da letto (f) *bed linen*
biancheria intima (f) *underwear*
bianco/a *white*
bibita (f) *drink (noun)*
bibite (f pl) *drinks*
biblioteca (f) *library*
bicchiere (m) *glass (drinking)*
bicicletta (f) *bicycle; exercise bike*

bidet (m) *bidet*
biglietteria (f) *ticket office*
biglietteria automatica (f) *automatic ticket machine*
biglietto (m) *ticket*
biglietto d'auguri (m) *card*
biglietto d'entrata (m) *entrance ticket*
biglietto di andata e ritorno (m) *return ticket*
biglietto di sola andata (m) *one-way ticket*
biglietto famiglia (m) *family ticket*
bikini (m) *bikini*
bilancia (f) *scale*
bimbo (m) *baby*
binario (m) *platform*
biondo *blonde*
birra (f) *beer*
biscotto (m) *cookie*
blatta (f) *cockroach*
blocco (m) *notebook*
blu *blue*
boa (f) *buoy*
bocca (f) *mouth*
boccaglio (m) *snorkel*
bollire *to boil*
bollitore (m) *camping kettle; kettle*
bonifico (m) *bank transfer*
bordo; a bordo *on board*
borraccia (f) *water bottle*
borsa (f) *bag; handbag*
borsa da viaggio (f) *duffel bag*
borsa per fotocamera (f) *camera bag*
bosco (m) *wood*
bottiglia (f) *bottle*
bottone (m) *button*
boutique (f) *boutique*
bowling (m) *bowling*
braccioli (m pl) *water wings*

braccio (m) *arm*
bretella (f) *entrance ramp*
brioche (f) *brioche*
britannico/a *British*
brocca (f) *pitcher*
broccolo (m) *broccoli*
bruciatura (f) *burn*
bruno/a *brunette*
brutto/a *ugly*
buffet (m) *buffet*
buffet della colazione (m)
 breakfast buffet
bulbo (m) *bulb*
Buon pomeriggio
 good afternoon
buonanotte *good night*
buonasera *good evening*
buongiorno *hello*
Buongiorno *good morning*
buono/a *good*
burro (m) *butter*
burro di arachidi (m)
 peanut butter
bussola (f) *compass*
busta (f) *envelope*
bustina di tè (f) *teabag*
busto (m) *bust*

C

cabina (f) *cabin*
cabina del telefono (f)
 telephone box
caffè (m) *coffee*
caffè nero (m) *black coffee*
caffettiera (f) *French press*
calcio (m) *soccer (game)*
calcio d'angolo (m) *corner*
calcolatrice (f) *calculator*
caldo/a *hot; warm*
calendario (m) *calendar*
calice da vino (m)
 wine glass
calmo/a *calm*

calzini (m pl) *socks*
calzoncini (m pl) *shorts*
cambiare *to change*
camera (f) *room*
camera a due letti (f)
 twin room
camera da letto (f)
 bedroom
camera doppia (f)
 double room
camera familiare (f)
 family room
camera singola (f)
 single room
cameriere/a *server*
camicetta (f) *blouse*
camicia (f) *shirt*
camminare *to walk*
campanello (m) *doorbell*
campeggiare *to camp*
campeggio (m) *campsite*
camper (m) *camper van*
campo (m) *field*
campo da golf (m)
 golf course
campo da tennis (m)
 tennis court
campo di cricket (m) *pitch*
Canada (m) *Canada*
canale di scolo (m) *drain*
canale (m) *channel (TV)*
cancello (m) *gate*
candeggina (f) *bleach*
cane (m) *dog*
canna da pesca (f)
 fishing rod
cannella (f) *cinnamon*
canoa (f) *canoe*
canottiera (f) *undershirt*
cantante (m/f) *singer*
cantiere (m) *construction site*
canzone (f) *song*
capelli (m pl) *hair*

capire *to understand*
capitale (f) *capital*
capo (m) *manager*
cappello (m) *hat*
cappello da sole (m)
    sunhat
cappotto (m) *coat*
cappuccino (m)
    cappuccino
cappuccio (m) *hood*
capsula (f) *capsule*
caramelle (f pl) *candy*
carburante (m) *gas*
cardigan (m) *cardigan*
caricare *to load*
carne (f) *meat*
carnevale (m) *carnival*
caro/a *expensive*
carota (f) *carrot*
carrello (m) *cart*
carrozza ristorante (f)
    dining car
carta assegni (f)
    check card
carta di credito (f)
    credit card
carta di debito (f)
    debit card
carta d'identità (f) *ID*
carta d'imbarco (f)
    boarding pass
carta igienica (f)
    toilet paper
carta studenti (f)
    student card
carta telefonica (f)
    phone card
cartelli stradali (m)
    road signs
carte (f pl) *cards*
cartello (m) *signpost*
cartina (f) *map; street map*
cartolina (f) *postcard*

cartone (m) *cardboard*
casa (f) *house*
cascata (f) *waterfall*
casco (m) *cycling helmet*
casinò (m) *casino*
cassa (f) *cash register*
cassa (f) *checkout
    (supermarket)*
casseruola (f) *casserole dish*
cassetta delle lettere (f)
    postbox
cassetta di pronto soccorso (f)
    first-aid box
cassetta per le lettere (f)
    letterbox
cassetto (m) *drawer*
cassiere/a (m/f) *checker*
castello (m) *castle*
casual *casual*
catamarano (m) *catamaran*
cattedrale (f) *cathedral*
cattivo/a *bad*
cavalletto (m) *bike rack*
cavallo (m) *horse*
cavatappi (m) *corkscrew*
caverna (f) *cave*
caviglia (f) *ankle*
cavolfiore (m) *cauliflower*
cavo (m) *cable*
cavolo (m) *cabbage*
CD (m) *CD*
c'è *there is*
ceci (m) *chickpeas*
cellulare (m) *cell phone*
cena (f) *dinner*
cento *hundred*
centro commerciale (m)
    shopping mall
centro della città (m) *town center*
centro sportivo (m)
    sports center
cercare *to search*
cerchio (m) *circle*

cereali da colazione (m) *breakfast cereals*
cerotto (m) *adhesive bandage*
certificato di nascita (m) *birth certificate*
cervello (m) *brain*
cestino (m) *trash*
cestino (m) *basket*
cestino da picnic (m) *picnic basket*
cetriolo (m) *cucumber*
champagne (m) *champagne*
check-in (m) *check in*
chi? *who?*
chiamata a carico del destinatario (f) *collect charge call*
chiave (f) *key*
chiave della camera (f) *room key*
chiavetta USB (f) *memory stick*
chicchi (m) *beans*
chiesa (f) *church*
chilogrammo (m) *kilogram*
chilo (m) *kilo*
chilometro (m) *kilometer*
chirurgo (m) *surgeon*
chiudere *to close*
chiudere a chiave *to lock*
chiuso/a *closed*
chiusura lampo (f) *zipper*
chorizo (m) *chorizo*
ci sono *there are*
ciao *hello*
ciascuno *each*
cibo (m) *food*
ciglio (m) *eyelash*
ciliegia (f) *cherry*
cin cin! *cheers!*
cinema (m) *movie theater*
cinquanta *fifty*
cinque *five*

cintura (f) *belt*
cioccolata calda (f) *hot chocolate*
cioccolatino (m) *chocolate*
cipolla (f) *onion*
circa *about*
citronella (f) *lemon grass*
città (f) *city; town*
clacson (m) *horn*
il/la cliente (m/f) *client*
clinica (f) *clinic*
cocktail (m) *cocktail*
cofano (m) *hood (car)*
coincidenza (f) *connection*
colazione (f) *breakfast*
coleottero (m) *beetle*
colino (m) *colander*
colla (f) *glue*
collana (f) *necklace*
collant (m) *panty hose*
collezione *collection*
collina (f) *hill*
collo (m) *neck*
collutorio (m) *mouthwash*
colori (m) *colors*
colpire *to knock down*
coltello (m) *knife*
come *as; how; like*
come? *how*
commesso/a (m/f) *sales assistant*
commissariato (m) *police station*
commissione bancaria (f) *bank charge*
compagno/a (m/f) *partner*
compartimento portabagagli (m) *overhead bin*
compleanno (m) *birthday*
completo (m) *suit*
comporre *to dial*
comprare *to buy*

comprendere *to understand*
compressa (f) *pill; tablet*
computer (m) *computer*
computer portatile (m)
    laptop
con *with*
concerto (m) *concert*
condominio (m)
    apartment block
confuso/a *confused*
congelato/a *frozen*
coniglio (m) *rabbit*
connettersi *to log on*
conoscere *to know (people)*
consigliare *to recommend*
consolato (m) *consulate*
console (m) *consul*
contare *to count*
contenitore (m) *container*
contenitore di riciclaggio
    (m) *recycling bin*
contento/a *happy*
contenuto (m) *contents*
continente (m) *continent*
conto (m) *check*
conto bancario (m)
    bank account
conto corrente (m)
    checking account
conto di risparmio (m)
    savings account
contorno (m) *side order*
contraccezione (f)
    contraception
controllo (m) *checkup*
controllo passaporti (m)
    passport control
controllore (m) *ticket inspector*
coperchio (m) *lid*
coperta (f) *blanket*
copiare *to copy*
coppia (f) *pair*
corda (f) *string*

coriandolo (m) *cilantro*
cornetto (m) *croissant*
cornice (f) *photo frame*
corpetto (m) *camisole*
corpo (m) *body*
corriere (m) *courier*
corsia (f) *aisle*
corsia (f) *ward*
cortile (m) *courtyard*
corto *short*
cosa? *what?*
così *so*
costa (f) *coast*
costola (f) *rib*
costoletta (f) *chop*
costruire *to build*
costume (m) *swimsuit*
cotone (m) *cotton*
crampo (m) *cramp*
cravatta (f) *tie*
crema (f) *cream*
crema per il corpo (f) *body lotion*
crema schermo totale (f) *sunblock*
crêpes (f pl) *crêpes*
cresta dell'onda (f) *surf*
crosta (f) *crust*
crudo *raw*
cruscotto (m) *dashboard*
cuccetta (f) *sleeper berth*
cucchiaino (m) *teaspoon*
cucchiaio (m) *spoon*
cucina (f) *kitchen*
cucinare *cooking*
cucire *to sew*
cuffia (f) *cap*
cuffie (f pl) *headphones*
cugino/a (m/f) *cousin*
cuocere al forno *to bake*
cuocere alla griglia *to broil*
cuoco/a (m/f) *chef*
cuore (m) *heart*
curry (m) *curry*
cuscino (m) *pillow*

custodia (f) *case*

D

da *by; from*
da asporto *take-away*
d'accordo *OK*
danneggiato/a *damaged*
danza (f) *ballet*
dare *to give*
dare la precedenza
 to give way
data di scadenza (f)
 sell-by date
davanti *front;*
 in front of; opposite
debole *weak*
decollare *to take off (clothes)*
delfino (m) *dolphin*
delizioso/a *delicious*
denaro (m) *cash; money*
dente (m) *tooth*
denti (m pl) *teeth*
dentifricio (m) *toothpaste*
dentista (m/f) *dentist*
dentro *into*
denuncia (f) *report (noun)*
denunciare *to report*
deodorante (m) *deodorant*
depilazione (f) *wax*
depositare *to deposit*
deposito (m) *deposit*
deposito bagagli (m)
 left luggage
derubare *to rob*
deserto (m) *desert*
dessert (m) *dessert*
destinazione (f) *destination*
destra: a destra *right (direction)*
detergente (m) *detergent*
detestare *to hate*
di *of; than*
diabetico/a *diabetic*
diarrea (f) *diarroea*

dicembre *December*
dichiarazione (f)
 statement
dieci *ten*
diesel *diesel*
diesis (m) *sharp*
dietro a *behind*
difficile *difficult*
digitare *to key*
dipartimento (m)
 department
dipinto (m) *painting*
dire *to say; to tell*
direttore della banca (m)
 bank manager
disabile (m) *disabled person*
discese per i principianti (f pl)
 green slopes
discipline (f pl) *events*
disco DVD (m) *DVD*
disconnettersi *to log out*
discutere *to discuss*
disegnare *to draw*
disegno (m) *drawing*
disinfettante (m) *antiseptic*
distanza (f) *distance*
distorsione (f) *sprain*
distretto (m) *district*
dito (m) *finger*
dito del piede (m) *toe*
ditta (f) *company*
divano (m) *sofa*
divano letto (m) *sofa bed*
divorziato/a *divorced*
dizionario (m) *dictionary*
doccia (f) *shower*
docciaschiuma (m)
 shower gel
documenti (m pl)
 papers (identity)
dodici *twelve*
dogana (f pl) *customs*
dolce *sweet; dessert*

dolcificante (m) *artificial sweetener*
dolciume (m) *snack bar*
dolore (m) *pain*
domani *tomorrow*
domenica *Sunday*
donna (f) *woman*
dopo *after*
doposole (m) *aftersun*
dormire *sleeping*
dorso del piede (m) *bridge*
dosaggio (m) *dosage*
dottore (m) *doctor*
dove? *where?*
dovere *to have to; must (verb)*
dritto (m) *straight*
due *two*
durante *during*
duro *hard*

E

e *and*
ecografia (f) *scan*
edicola (f) *newsstand*
effetto indesiderato (m) *side effect*
effettuare un deposito *to pay in*
egli *he*
elettricista (m) *electrician*
elettricità (f) *electricity*
ella *she*
ellittica (f) *cross trainer*
e-mail (f) *email*
ematoma (m) *bruise*
emergenza (f) *emergency*
emicrania (f) *migraine*
emigrare *to emigrate*
entrata (f) *entrance*
entusiasta *excited*
epilettico/a *epileptic*

erba aromatica (f) *herb*
errore (m) *mistake*
eruzione (f) *rash*
esaminare *to examine*
esattamente *exactly*
esatto/a *right (correct)*
escoriazione (f) *graze*
escursione a cavallo (f) *trekking*
escursionismo (m) *hiking*
esposizione (f) *exhibition*
espresso (m) *espresso*
espulsione (f) *send off*
essere *to be*
essere in debito *to owe*
esso/a *it*
est (m) *east*
estate (f) *summer*
estintore (m) *fire extinguisher*
etichette (f pl) *labels*
euro (m) *euro*
extra *extra*

F

facchino (m) *porter*
facile *easy*
famiglia (f) *family*
fard (m) *blush*
fare *to do; to make*
fare il check-in *to check in*
fare la spesa *to go shopping*
fare le valigie *to pack*
fare marcia indietro *to reverse*
fare surf *to surf*
fari (m pl) *headlights*
farmacia (f) *pharmacy*
farmacista (m) *pharmacist*
faro (m) *lighthouse*
fasciatura (f) *dressing*
fast food (m) *fast food*
fattoria (f) *farm*

fazzolettino (m) *tissue*
febbraio *February*
febbre (f) *fever*
felice *happy*
felpa (f) *sweatshirt*
ferita (f) *injury*
fermare *to stop*
fermata dell'autobus (f)
  bus stop
ferramenta (f)
  hardware store
ferrovia (f) *railroad*
festa (f) *celebration*
feste (f pl) *festivals*
fetta (f) *slice*
fiammifero (m)
  match (light)
fibbia (f) *buckle*
fidanzata (f) *girlfriend*
fidanzato (m) *boyfriend*
fiero/a *proud*
figlia (f) *daughter*
figlio (m) *son*
fila (f) *row*
filetto (m) *fillet*
film (m) *movie*
filone (m) *baguette*
filtro solare (m)
  sunscreen
fine (f) *end*
fine settimana (m)
  weekend
finestra (f) *window*
finire *to finish*
fino a *until*
fioraio/a (m/f) *florist*
fiore (m) *club*
fiori (m pl) *flowers*
firma (f) *signature*
firmare *to sign*
fitness (m) *fitness*
fiume (m) *river*
flash (m) *flash gun*

fontana (f) *fountain*
footing (m) *jogging*
forbici (f pl) *scissors*
forbicine per le unghie (f pl)
  nail scissors
forchetta (f) *fork*
foresta (f) *forest*
foresta pluviale (f) *rain forest*
formaggio (m) *cheese*
formaggio cremoso (m)
  cream cheese
fornetto da campeggio (m)
  camping stove
forno (m) *oven*
forno a microonde (m)
  microwave
forse *perhaps*
forte *strong*
fotocamera digitale (f)
  digital camera
fotocamera (f) *camera*
fotografia (f) *photograph*
fotografia (sviluppata) (f)
  print
fotografia con il flash (f)
  flash photography
fragile *fragile*
fragola (f) *strawberry*
francobollo (m) *stamp*
fratello (m) *brother*
frattura (f) *fracture*
frecce lampeggianti (f pl)
  hazard lights
freddo/a *cold*
freno (m) *brake*
fresco/a *fresh*
friggere *to fry*
frigo portatile (m) *cooler*
frigorifero (m) *refrigerator*
frigorifero congelatore (m)
  side-by-side refrigerator
frittata (f) *omelet*
fritto *fried*

fritto in olio abbondante *deep-fried*
fritto in padella *pan fried*
frittura (f) *stir-fry*
fronte; di fronte a *front; in front of; opposite*
frullatore (m) *blender*
frusta (f) *whisk*
frutta (f) *fruit*
frutti di mare (m) *seafood*
fruttivendolo (m) *produce seller*
fumare *to smoke*
fumetto (m) *comic book*
fumo (m) *smoke*
fungo (m) *mushroom*
funivia (f) *cable car*
funzionare *to work (machine)*
fuori *outside*
furto (m) *robbery*

G

galleria (f) *gallery (theater)*
galleria d'arte (f) *art gallery*
galosce (f pl) *rain boots*
gamba (f) *leg*
gara (f) *race*
garage (m) *garage*
garanzia (f) *guarantee*
gas (m) *gas*
gastronomia (f) *delicatessen*
gatto (m) *cat*
gelato/a (m/f) *freeze*
gelo (m) *frost*
gemelli (m pl) *cufflinks*
generalmente *usually*
genitori (m pl) *parents*
gennaio *January*
gente (f) *people*
ghiacciato/a *icy*
ghiaccio (m) *ice*
già *already*

giacca (f) *jacket*
giaccone (m) *parka*
giallo/a *yellow*
giardino (m) *garden*
gin (m) *gin*
ginocchiere (f pl) *pads*
ginocchio (m) *knee*
giocare *to play (games)*
giocattolo (m) *toy*
gioco (m) *game*
gioielleria (f) *jewely*
gioielliere (m) *jeweler*
giornale (m) *newspaper*
giorno (m) *day*
giorno festivo (m) *public holiday*
giostre (f pl) *rides*
giovane *young*
giovedì *Thursday*
giraffa (f) *giraffe*
giro (m) *run*
giro (m) *tour*
giro turistico (m) *sightseeing*
gita (f) *trip*
giù *down*
giubbotto di salvataggio (m) *life jacket*
giugno *June*
giunco (m) *rush*
giusto/a *right (correct)*
gli *the (m pl)*
gola (f) *throat*
golf (m) *golf*
gomito (m) *elbow*
gomma a terra (f) *puncture*
gomma da masticare (f) *chewing gum*
gonna (f) *skirt*
gradi *degrees*
grammo (m) *gram*
Gran Bretagna (f) *Great Britain*
granchio (m) *crab*
grande *big; large*

grande magazzino (m)
   department store
grandine (f) *hail*
grano (m) *wheat*
grasso (m) *fat*
gratis *free (no charge)*
grattugia (f) *grater*
grave *serious*
grazie *thank you*
grembiule (m) *apron*
gridare *to shout*
grigio *gray*
griglia (f) *griddle pan*
griglia per barbecue (f)
   barbecue
gruppo (m) *group*
guancia (f) *cheek*
guanti (m pl) *gloves*
guanti da forno (m pl)
   oven mitts
guanto da baseball (m)
   baseball glove
guardacoste (m) *coastguard*
guardare *to look; to watch*
guasto (m) *breakdown*
guida (f) *guide; guidebook*
guida turistica (f) *tour guide*
guidare *to drive*

H, I, J, K

hamburger (m) *burger*
hamburger vegetariano (m)
   veggie burger
hockey (m) *hockey*
hovercraft (m) *hovercraft*
i *the (m pl)*
ieri *yesterday*
idrante (m) *fire hydrant*
isola (f) *island*
idraulico (m) *plumber*
il *the (m)*
imbarazzata *embarrassed*
imbarcarsi *to board*

imbarcazione da diporto
   (f) *pleasure boat*
immigrazione (f)
   immigration
imparare *to learn*
impianto di riscaldamento
   (m) *heater*
impianto stereo dell' automobile
   (m) *car stereo*
importo (m) *amount*
imposta (f) *tax*
imputazione (f) *charge*
in *in*
in stato interessante *pregnant*
inalatore (m) *inhaler*
incartare *to gift-wrap*
incassare *to cash*
incendio (m) *fire*
incidente (m) *accident*
incidente stradale (m)
   car accident
incinta *pregnant*
incisione (f) *engraving*
indicatore di livello del
   carburante (m) *fuel gauge*
Indicazioni (f) *directions*
indirizzo (m) *address*
indirizzo e-mail (m)
   email address
indumenti impermeabili
   (m pl) *slickers*
infermiere/a (m/f) *nurse*
infezione (f) *infection*
infiammato/a *sore*
influenza (f) *the flu*
infradito (f) *flip-flop*
infreddatura (f) *chill*
inglese *English*
ingorgo (m) *traffic jam*
Ingresso vietato (m)
   no entry
iniezione (f) *injection*
inizio (m) *beginning*

inondazione (f) *flood*
insalata (f) *salad*
insalatiera (f) *mixing bowl*
insegna (f) *sign*
interessante *interesting*
interessare *to interest*
Internet (m) *internet*
Internet cafè (m) *internet café*
intero *whole*
interprete (m/f) *interpreter*
interruttore (m) *switch*
interruttore per le luci (m)
    lights switch
interruzione di corrente (f)
    power outage
intervento chirurgico (m)
    operation (medical)
inventario (m) *inventory*
inverno (m) *winter*
inviare *to send*
io *I*
istruzioni (f pl)
    instructions
iPod (m) *iPod*
ippodromo (m)
    racecourse
Italia (f) *Italy*
italiano/a *Italian*
jazz club (m) *jazz club*
jeans (m pl) *jeans*
kayak (m) *kayak*
ketchup (m) *ketchup*

L

la *the (f)*
là *over there*
ladro (m) *thief*
lago (m) *lake*
lampadina (f) *light bulb*
lampone (m) *raspberry*
lana (f) *wool*
larghezza (f) *width*
largo *wide*

lasciare *to check out*
    (hotel); to leave; to vacate
lassù *up there*
lato (m) *side*
latte (m) *milk*
latticini (m pl) *dairy produce*
lattuga (f) *lettuce*
lavanderia (f) *laundromat*
lavandino (m) *sink*
lavare *to wash*
lavastoviglie (f) *dishwasher*
lavatrice (f) *washing machine*
lavorare *to work*
lavori stradali (m)
    roadwork
lavoro (m) *work;*
    per lavoro *on business*
le *the (f pl)*
leggere *to read*
leggero/a *light*
le *her (object)*
lei *she;* **Lei** *you*
lente (f) *lens*
lenti a contatto (f pl)
    contact lenses
lento/a *slow*
lenzuolo (m) *sheet*
lettino (m) *crib*
lettino sdraio (m)
    lounge chair
lettino solare (m) *sunbed*
letto (m) *bed*
letto matrimoniale (m)
    double bed
letto singolo (m) *single bed*
lettore CD (m) *CD player*
lettore DVD (m) *DVD player*
leva del cambio (f) *gear shift*
libbra (f) *pound*
libero/a *free (not occupied)*
libreria (f) *bookstore*
libretto degli assegni (m)
    checkbook

libro (m) *book*
lievitare *to prove*
limite di velocità (m)
   speed limit
limonata (f) *lemonade*
limone (m) *lemon*
linea (f) *line*
lingua (f) *tongue*
liquido *liquid*
lista (f) *list*
lista dei vini (f) *wine list*
listino (m) *price list*
litro (m) *liter*
lo *the (m)*
locale *local*
lontano *far*
loro *their; they*
lozione solare (f)
   suntan lotion
lucchetto (m) *lock*
luce (f) *light (noun)*
luce del sole (f) *sunshine*
lucido *gloss*
luglio *July*
lui *he; him*
luna park (m) *fairground*
lunedì *Monday*
lunghezza (f) *length*
lungo/a *long*
luoghi d'interesse (m pl)
   attractions
luogo (m) *place*
luogo d'interesse turistico
   (m) *tourist attraction*

M

macchina (f) *car; machine*
macchina del caffè (f)
   coffee machine
macelleria (f) *butcher*
macinato (?) *ground*
madre (f) *mother*
maggio *May*

maglio (m) *mallet*
maglione (m) *sweater*
mai *never*
maiale (m) *pork*
maionese (f) *mayonnaise*
mais (m) *corn*
mal di denti (m) *toothache*
mal di stomaco
   stomach ache
mal di testa (m) *headache*
malato/a *sick*
malattia (f) *illness*
mandare *to send*
mangiare *to eat*
mangiare fuori *eating out*
mangiare sul posto *eat-in*
mango (m) *mango*
manicure (f) *manicure*
maniglia (f) *handle*
mano (f) *hand*
manoscritto (m) *manuscript*
manzo (m) *beef*
mappa (f) *map; street map*
mappa della metropolitana
   (f) *subway map*
marciapiede (m) *sidewalk*
mare (m) *sea*
marito (m) *husband*
marmellata (f) *jam*
marmellata di agrumi (f)
   marmalade
marmitta (f) *exhaust (car)*
marrone *brown*
martedì *Tuesday*
marzo *March*
mascara (m) *mascara*
mascella (f) *jaw*
massaggio (m) *massage*
materasso (m) *mattress*
matita (f) *pencil*
matita per gli occhi (f)
   eyeliner
matrimonio (m) *wedding*

mattino (m) *morning*
mattone (m) *brick*
maturo/a *ripe*
mazza (f) *golf club*
mazzetto (m) *bunch*
mazzo di carte (m)
  pack of cards
meccanico (m) *mechanic*
medicina (f) *medicine*
medicina per la tosse (f)
  cough medicine
medusa (f) *jellyfish*
mela (f) *apple*
melanzana (f) *eggplant*
meno *less*
mensola (f) *shelves*
menta (f) *mint*
mento (m) *chin*
menù (m) *menu*
menù della cena (m)
  evening menu
menù del pranzo (m)
  lunch menu
mercato (m) *market*
mercoledì *Wednesday*
merluzzo (m) *cod*
mese (m) *month*
messaggio (m) *message*
messaggio vocale (m)
  voice message
metà *half*
meta (f) *try*
metallo (m) *metal*
metro (m) *meter*
metropolitana (f)
  subway
mettere *to put*
mezzanotte *midnight*
mezzo *medium;*
  middle; half
mezzogiorno *noon*
mi scusi *excuse me*
mia/mie *my (f/f pl))*

miglio (m) *mile*
migliore *better*
minestra (f) *soup*
minestrone (m) *stew*
mini bar (m) *mini bar*
minuto (m) *minute*
mio/miei *my (m/m pl))*
mirtillo (m) *blueberry*
misto/a *mixed*
misura (f) *measure*
moda (f) *fashion*
modulo (m) *form*
moglie (f) *wife*
molti/e *many*
moltissimo *very much*
molto *much; very*
moneta (f) *coin*
montagna (f) *mountain*
monumento (m)
  monument
mora (f) *blackberry*
morbido *soft*
morso (m) *bite*
mossa (f) *move*
moto d'acqua (m) *jet ski*
motocicletta (f) *motorcycle*
motore (m) *engine*
mountain bike (f)
  mountain bike
mouse (m)
  mouse (computer)
mozzarella (f)
  mozzarella
mucca (f) *cow*
muffin (m) *muffin*
multa (f) *fine (legal)*
municipio (m) *town hall*
muratore (m) *construction worker*
muro (m) *wall*
muscoli (m pl) *muscles*
museo (m) *museum*
musica (f) *music*
musica da ballo (f) *dance*

musicista (m) *musician*

N

nascita (f) *birth*
naso (m) *nose*
naturale *natural*
nausea (f) *nausea*
navigare *to navigate*
navigatore satellitare (m)
   GPS receiver
navigazione via satellite
   (f) *satellite navigation*
nebbia (f) *fog*
nebbioso/a *misty*
negozio (m) *store*
negozio di arredamento (m)
   furniture store
negozio di articoli da regalo
   (m) *gift store*
negozio di calzature (m)
   shoe store
negozio di dischi
   record store
negozio duty-free (m)
   duty-free store
neo (m) *mole (medical)*
nero/a *black*
nervosa *nervous*
neve (f) *snow*
niente *anything; nothing*
nightclub (m) *nightclub*
no *no*
noccioline (f pl) *nuts*
noce di cocco (f) *coconut*
noi *us; we*
noleggiare *to hire; to rent*
nome (m) *name*
non *not*
nord (m) *north*
normale *normal*
nostro/nostri/
   nostra/nostre *our*
nota (f) *note*

notte (f) *night*
nove *nine*
novembre *November*
numero (m) *number*
numero del volo (m)
   flight number
numero di conto (m)
   account number
numero di targa (m)
   registration number
numero di telefono (m)
   contact number
nuotare *to swim*
nuoto (m) *swimming*
nuoto subacqueo (m)
   scuba diving
nuovo/a *new*
nuvola (f) *cloud*
nuvoloso/a *cloudy*

O

o *or*
occhiali (m pl) *glasses*
occhiali da sole (m pl)
   sunglasses
occhialini (m pl) *goggles*
occhio (m) *eye*
occupato *engaged/busy*
oceano *ocean*
odiare *to hate*
oggetti di valore (m pl)
   valuables
oggi *today*
ogni *each (every)*
olio (m) *oil*
olio di semi di girasole (m)
   sunflower oil
olio d'oliva (m) *olive oil*
olive (f pl) *olives*
oltre *beyond*
ombrello (m) *umbrella*
ombrellone da spiaggia (m)
   beach umbrella

onda (f) *wave*
online *online*
opaco/a *matte*
opera (f) *opera*
opera teatrale (f) *play*
ora (f) *hour*
orario (m) *timetable*
orario delle visite (m) *visiting hours*
orario di apertura (m) *opening hours*
oratrice (f) *speaker*
ordinare *to order*
ordine (m) *order*
orecchino *earrings*
orecchio (m) *ear*
ormeggio (m) *mooring*
oro *gold*
orologio *clock*
orologio da polso (m) *wrist watch*
orribile *awful*
orso *bear*
ospedale (m) *hospital*
ospite (f/m) *guest*
otto *eight*
ottobre *October*
ovest (m) *west*
ovulo *egg*

P

pacchetto (m) *packet*
pacco (m) *package*
padella (f) *frying pan*
padre (m) *father*
padrone di casa (m) *host*
paese (m) *country; village*
pagamento (m) *payment*
pagare *to pay*
pagare in contanti *to pay cash*
palcoscenico (m) *stage*
palestra (f) *gym*
paletta (f) *dust pan*

palla (f) *ball*
palla da golf (f) *golf ball*
palla da tennis (f) *tennis balll*
pallina (f) *scoop*
pallone da spiaggia (m) *beach ball*
pallone (m) *soccer (ball)*
panca (f) *bench*
pancetta (f) *bacon*
pane (m) *bread*
pane nero (m) *whole-wheat bread*
pane tostato (m) *toast*
panetteria (f) *bakery*
panificio (m) *bakery*
panne; in panne *broken (in car)*
pannolino (m) *diaper*
pantaloni (m pl) *pants*
pantofole (f pl) *slippers*
pappa d'avena (f) *porridge*
parabrezza (m) *windshield*
parare *to save*
parata (f) *block*
paraurti (m) *bumper*
parcheggiare *to park*
parcheggio (m) *parking*
parcheggio per disabili (m) *disabled parking*
parchimetro (m) *parking meter*
parco (m) *park*
parco a tema (m) *theme park*
parco nazionale (m) *national park*
parco safari (m) *safari park*
parenti (m pl) *relatives*
parlare *to speak*
parmigiano (m) *parmesan*
parrucchiere/a (m/f) *hairdresser's*
partecipare *to attend*
partenze (f pl) *departures*
parte posteriore (f) *back (not front of)*
partire *to depart; to leave*
partita (f) *match (sport)*
parto (m) *delivery*

pass per lo ski-lift (m) *lift pass*
passaggio (m) *pass*
passaporto (m) *passport*
passeggero (m) *passenger*
passeggiata (f) *walk*
passo (m) *walk*
pasta (f) *pasta*
paste (f pl) *pastry*
pasticca per la gola (f)
  throat lozenge
pasticche antinausea (f pl)
  travel-sickness pills
pasticcio (m) *pie*
pastina (f) *bun*
pasto a bordo (m) *in-flight meal*
patata (f) *potato*
patata dolce (f) *sweet potato*
patatine (f pl) *potato chips*
patente di guida (f) *driver's license*
patologia cardiaca (f)
  heart condition
pattinaggio su ghiaccio (m)
  ice-skating
pattino (m) *skate*
pattumiera (f) *garbage can*
pausa (f) *rest*
pavimento (m) *floor*
paziente (m/f) *patient*
pedaggio (m) *toll*
pedicure (f) *pedicure*
pedina (f) *tile*
peggiore *worse*
pelle (f) *skin*
peluche (m) *stuffed animal*
pendice (f) *slope*
penna (f) *pen*
pensare *to think*
pensione; in pensione *retired*
pensione con colazione (f)
  bed and breakfast
pentola (f) *saucepan*
pepe (m) *pepper*
peperoncino (m) *chili pepper*

per *for*
pera (f) *pear*
perché? *why?*
perdere *to lose*
perdita (f) *leak*
per favore *please*
pericolo *danger*
periferia (f) *suburb*
personale (m) *staff*
persone (f pl) *people*
pesante *heavy*
pesare *to weigh*
pesce (m) *fish*
pescivendolo (m) *fish seller*
peso (m) *weight*
pettine (m) *comb*
pezzo (m) *piece*
piacere *to like*
piacevole *nice*
pialla (f) *plane*
pianeta (m) *planet*
piangere *to cry*
pianista (m/f) *pianist*
piantare una tenda
  to pitch a tent
piante (f pl) *plants*
piattino (m) *saucer; side plate*
piatto (m) *dish; plate*
piatto principale (m)
  main course
piazza (f) *square (in town)*
piccante *hot (spicy)*
picchetto (m) *tent peg*
piccolo/a *small; little*
picnic (m) *picnic*
piede (m) *foot*
pieno/a *full*
pietra preziosa (f) *stone*
pigiama (m) *pajamas*
pilates *pilates*
pilota (m/f) *pilot*
PIN (m) *PIN*
pinne (f pl) *fins*

pinta (f) *pint*
pinzetta (f) *tweezers*
piove *to rain*
piovra (m); polpo (m) *octopus*
piscina (f) *swimming pool*
pista ciclabile (f) *cycle lane*
pista da sci (f) *ski slope*
più *more*
piumone (m) *comforter*
pizza (f) *pizza*
platea (f) *stalls*
pneumatico (m) *tire*
poco *little*
poggiatesta (m) *head rest*
poi *then*
polizia (f) *police*
poliziotta (f) *policewoman*
poliziotto (m) *policeman*
polizza assicurativa (f)
   insurance policy
polizza (f) *policy*
pollame (m) *poultry*
pollice (m) *thumb*
pollo (m) *chicken*
polpette (f pl) *meatballs*
polso (m) *wrist*
polvere (f) *powder*
pomata (f) *ointment*
pomeriggio (m) *afternoon*
pomodoro (m) *tomato*
pomodoro ciliegino (m)
   cherry tomato
pompa (f) *pump*
pompiere (m) *firefighter*
portabagagli (m) *luggage rack*
porta (f) *door*
portafoglio (m) *wallet*
portamonete (m) *change purse*
portare *to carry;* **da portar via**
   takeaway
portate (f pl) *courses*
portellone (m) *hatchback*
porticciolo (m) *marina*

porto (m) *harbor*
portone (m) *front door*
porzione (f) *portion*
posacenere (m) *ashtray*
posate (f pl) *cutlery*
possibile *possible*
posta *mail*
posta aerea (f) *airmail*
posta in arrivo (f) *inbox*
posteggio dei taxi (m) *taxi stand*
postino (m) *letter carrier*
posto (m) *place; seat*
posto vicino al corridoio (m)
   aisle seat
posto vicino al finestrino (m)
   window seat
potere *can (verb)*
pranzo (m) *lunch*
preferito/a *favourite*
prelevare *to withdraw (money)*
prelievo (m) *withdrawal*
prendere *to take/to catch*
prendere il sole *to sunbathe*
prendere in prestito *to borrow*
prenotare *to book; reserve*
prenotare un volo *to book a flight*
prenotazione (f) *reservation*
preoccupato/a *worried*
preservativo (m) *condom*
pressione arteriosa elevata (f)
   high blood pressure
pressione degli pneumatici (f) *tire
   pressure*
prestito (m) *loan*
presto *early; soon*
prezzemolo (m) *parsley*
prezzo (m) *price*
prima di *before*
primato (m) *record*
primavera (f) *spring*
primo/a *first*
primo piano (m) *second floor*
principiante (m/f) *beginner*

profumo (m) *perfume*
proiezione (f) *throw*
prolunga (f) *extension cord*
pronto/a *ready*
pronto soccorso (m) *emergency room*
Pronto Soccorso (m) *accident and emergency*
prossimo/a *next*
provare *to try*
provincia (f) *province*
prugna (f) *plum*
pubblico (m) *audience*
pulire *to wipe*
pulito/a *clean*
pullman (m) *coach*
pullman turistico (m) *tour bus*
pulsante di chiamata (m) *call button*
pungiglione (m) *sting*
punta (f) *tip*
punto (m) *point*

Q

quadrato (m) *square*
qualche volta *sometimes*
qualcosa *anything*
qualcosa *something*
qualcuno/a *somebody*
quale? *which?*
quando? *when?*
quanti/e? *how many?*
quanto? *how much?*
quaranta *forty*
quasi *almost*
quattordici *fourteen*
quattro *four*
quello/a *that*
questo/a *this*
qui *here*
quindici *fifteen*
quindici giorni *fortnight*
quota (f) *altitude*

R

racchetta da tennis (f) *tennis racket*
racchette da sci (f pl) *ski poles*
radiatore (m) *radiator*
radice (f) *root*
radio (f) *radio*
radio digitale (f) *digital radio*
radiografia (f) *X-ray*
radiosveglia (f) *clock radio*
raffreddore (m) *cold (illness)*
raffreddore da fieno (m) *hay fever*
ragazzo/a (m/f) *boy/girl*
raggio (m) *spoke*
ragno (m) *spider*
rallentare *slow down*
ramo (m) *branch*
rampa di accesso (f) *slip road*
rampa per i disabili (f) *wheelchair ramp*
rapido/a *quick*
raramente *rarely*
rasoio (m) *razor*
rasoio elettrico (m) *electric razor*
rastrelliera (f) *rack*
ratto (m) *rat*
reato (m) *crime*
recinto (m) *fence*
reclamare *to complain*
reffreddore da fieno (m) *hay fever*
regalo (m) *gift; present*
regione (f) *region*
rene (m) *kidney (medical)*
reparto di terapia intensiva (m) *intensive care unit*
repellente per gli insetti (m) *insect repellent*
rete (f) *network*
retro (m) *back (not front of)*
rianimazione (f) *resuscitation*
riavviare *to reboot*
riavvolgimento (m) *rewind*

ribes nero (m) *blackcurrant*
riccio *curly*
ricerca (f) *research*
ricetta medica (f) *prescription*
ricevere *to receive*
ricevuta (f) *receipt*
ricevuta dei bagagli (f)
  reclaim tag
ricezione (f) *reception*
ricordi (m pl) *souvenirs*
ridere *to laugh*
riduzione (f) *reduction*
riempire *to fill*
rilasciare *to release*
rimestare *to stir*
rimorchiare *to tow*
riparare *to fix; repair*
riparazione (f) *repair*
riscaldamento centralizzato
  (m) *central heating*
riscaldamento (m) *heating*
riscuotere *to cash*
riservare *to reserve*
riso (m) *rice*
riso integrale (m) *brown rice*
rispondere *to answer*
ristorante (m) *restaurant*
ritardo; in ritardo *late*
ritiro bagagli (m) *baggage claim*
ritorno (m) *return*
rivelatore di fumo (m)
  smoke alarm
rivista (f) *magazine*
rocce (f pl) *rocks*
rosa *pink*
rosolare *to sauté*
rosso/a *red*
rotaia (f) *rail*
rotatoria (f) *traffic circle*
rotondo/a *round*
rotto/a *broken*
rough (m) *rough*
router (f) *router*

rubato/a *stolen*
rubinetto (m) *faucet*
rubinetto di arresto (m)
  water valve
rubino (m) *ruby*
rullino (m) *roll (of film)*
rumoroso *noisy*
ruota (f) *tire; wheel*
ruota di scorta (f) *spare tire*
russare *to snore*

S

sabato *Saturday*
sabbia (f) *sand*
sacca da viaggio (f) *holdall*
sacco a pelo (m) *sleeping bag*
sala da pranzo (f) *dining room*
sala d'attesa (f) *waiting room*
sala delle partenze (f)
  departure lounge
salame (m) *salami*
salato *salted*
sale (m) *salt*
salmone (m) *salmon*
salotto (m) *living room*
salsa (f) *sauce*
salute (f) *health*
salvagente (m) *life ring*
salviettina umidificata (f)
  wet wipe
sandali (m pl) *sandals*
sangue dal naso (m) *nosebleed*
sapere *to know (a fact)*
sapone (m) *soap*
sarto (m) *tailor*
sauna (f) *sauna*
sbagliato/a *wrong*
sbarcare *to disembark*
sbucciare *to peel*
sbucciatore (m) *peeler*
scaffale (m) *shelf*
scala (f) *staircase*
scala di sicurezza (f) *fire escape*

scale (f pl) *stairs*

scaricare *to download*

scarpa (f) *shoe*

scarpe (f pl) *shoes*

scarpe da ginnastica (f pl)
  sneakers

scarpone (m) *boot*

scarponi (m pl) *hiking boots*

scarponi da sci (m pl) *ski boots*

scatola (f) *box*

scatola dei fusibili (f) *fuse box*

scatoletta (f) *can (noun)*

scendere *to get off*

scenografia (f) *set*

scheda del paziente (f) *chart*

scheda di memoria (f)
  memory card

scheggia (f) *splinter*

schiacciata (f) *smash*

schiena (f) *back (body)*

schienale (m) *back*

schiuma da barba (f)
  shaving foam

schizzo (m) *sketch*

sci (m) *skiing*

sci (m pl) *skis*

sciacquare *to rinse*

sciarpa (f) *scarf*

sci d'acqua (m) *water-skiing*

scimmia (f) *monkey*

scivolo (m) *slide*

scodella (f) *bowl*

scogliera (f) *cliff*

scompartimento (m)
  compartment

scopa (f) *brush (cleaning)*

scoperto (m) *overdraft*

scotch (m) *adhesive tape*

scottatura solare (f) *sunburn*

scrivania (f) *desk*

scrivere *to write*

scuola (f) *school*

scuro/a *dark*

scusi *sorry*

secchio (m) *bucket*

secco/a *dry (wine)*

secondo/a *second*

secondo piano (m) *third floor*

sedia a rotelle (f) *wheelchair*

sedia a sdraio (f) *deck chair*

sedia (f) *chair*

seggiolino (m) *child seat*

seggiolone (m) *high chair*

seggiovia (f) *chair lift*

segnale (m) *signal*

segnale stradale (m) *street sign*

segnali stradali (m pl) *road signs*

sei *six*

semaforo (m) *traffic lights*

semi (m pl) *seeds*

seminterrato (m) *basement*

sempre *always*

senape (f) *mustard*

sensibile *sensitive*

sentenza (f) *sentence*

sentiero (m) *footpath*

sentire *to hear*

senza *without*

senza piombo *unleaded*

senza semi *seedless*

separatamente *separately*

sera (f) *evening*

serbatoio (m) *tank*

serpente (m) *snake*

servizi di emergenza (m pl)
  emergency services

servizio di babysitting (m)
  babysitting

servizio espresso (m)
  express service

servizio (m) *serve*

seta (f) *silk*

sette *seven*

settembre *September*

settimana (f) *week*

settimana prossima (f) *next week*
settimana scorsa (f) *last week*
shampoo (m) *shampoo*
shock (m) *shock*
sì *yes*
sicuro/a di sé *confident*
sicurezza (f) *security*
sicuro/a *safe*
sigaretta (f) *cigarette*
sigarette (f pl) *cigarettes*
sigaro (m) *cigar*
sinistra (f) *left*
sipario (m) *curtain*
sirena (f) *siren*
sito web (m) *website*
slip (m) *briefs*
smartphone (m) *smartphone*
snowboard (m) *snowboarding*
soda (f) *soda water*
soffitto (m) *ceiling*
soffocare *to choke*
soggiorno (m) *stay*
solamente *only*
soldi (m pl) *money*
sole (m) *sun*
solito/a *usual*
solo/a *alone*
sommare *to add*
sonnifero (m) *sleeping pill*
sopra *above*
sopra *over*
sopracciglio (m) *eyebrow*
sorbetto (m) *sherbet*
sorella (f) *sister*
sorgere del sole (m) *sunrise*
sorpassare *to pass*
sorpreso/a *surprised*
sorriso (m) *smile*
sostegno (m) *stand*
sottile *thin*
sotto *below; beneath*
sottobicchiere (m) *coaster*
sottopassaggio (m) *underpass*

sottoveste (f) *slip*
souvenir (m) *souvenir*
spalla (f) *shoulder*
spallina (f) *strap*
spartito (m) *score*
spatola (f) *spatula*
spaventato/a *scared*
spazio con fasciatoio (m)
  baby changing room
spazzare *to sweep*
spazzola (f) *brush*
spazzolino da denti (m)
  toothbrush
specchio (m) *mirror*
specialità (f) *speciality*
spedire *to send*
spedire la posta *to mail*
spegnere *to turn off*
spento/a *off*
spesa (f) *groceries*
spesso *often*
spezie (f pl) *spices*
spiaggia (f) *beach*
spina (f) *plug*
spina dorsale (f) *spine*
spinaci (m pl) *spinach*
spingere *push*
spogliatoio (m) *fitting room*
sporco *dirty*
sport (m) *sport*
sport acquatici (m pl) *watersports*
sportello bancomat (m)
  cash machine
sport invernali (m pl)
  winter sports
sposato/a *married*
spray (m) *spray*
spugna (f) *sponge*
spuntino (m) *snack*
squadra (f) *team*
squalo (m) *shark*
stagione (f) *season*
stagioni (f pl) *seasons*

stampa (f) *print (photo)*
stampare *to print*
stanza libera (f) *vacancy (room)*
starnutire *to sneeze*
starnuto (m) *sneeze*
stasera *tonight*
Stati Uniti (m pl) *United States*
statua (f) *statue*
stazione (f) *train station*
stazione degli autobus (f)
  bus station
stazione di servizio (f)
  gas station
stazione ferroviaria (f)
  train station
stecca (f) *splint*
step machine (f) *step machine*
sterlina (f) *sterling*
stesso/a *same*
stitichezza (f) *constipation*
stivale (m) *boot*
stomaco (m) *stomach*
stop (m) *stop*
strada (f) *road; street; way*
strade (f pl) *roads*
stress (m) *stress*
stretto/a *tight*
struttura (f) *frame*
studente/studentessa (m/f)
  student
studio (m) *study*
stuzzichini (m pl) *bar snacks*
su *on; over; up*
succedere *to happen*
succo (m) *juice*
succo d'arancia (m) *orange juice*
succo di mela (m) *apple juice*
sud (m) *south*
suo/suoi/sua/sue *his; her*
superficie (f) *area*
supermercato (m) *supermarket*
supporto (m) *support*
supposte (f pl) *suppositories*

svaligiare *to burgle*
sveglia (f) *alarm clock*
svegliarsi *to wake up (oneself)*
sveglia telefonica (f) *wake-up call*
svenire *to faint*
sviluppare *to develop (film)*

T

tabaccaio (m) *tobacconist*
tabacco (m) *tobacco*
tabellone (m) *bulletin board*
tachimetro (m) *speedometer*
taglia (f) *size*
tagliaunghie (m) *nail clippers*
tagliere (m) *cutting board*
taglio (m) *cut*
tallone (m) *heel*
tampone (m) *tampon*
tappeto (m) *rug*
tappo (m) *cork*
tardi *late*
tariffa (f) *fare*
tasca (f) *pocket*
tassista (m) *taxi driver*
tasso di cambio (m)
  exchange rate
tastiera (f) *keyboard*
tavola da surf (f) *windsurf board*
tavoletta (f) *float*
tavolino (m) *coffee table*
tavolo (m) *table*
taxi (m) *taxi*
tazza (f) *cup*
tazzina da caffè (f) *coffee cup*
teatro (m) *theater*
teatro dell'opera (m)
  opera house
teglia da forno (f) *cookie sheet*
teiera (f) *teapot*
telecomando (m) *remote control*
telefonare *to telephone*
telefonata (f) *phone call*
telefono (m) *telephone*

telefono pubblico (m)
payphone
telegiornale (m) *news*
televisione via cavo (f)
cable television
televisore (m) *television*
**televisore a schermo panoramico
(m)** *widescreen TV*
telo da spiaggia (m)
beach towel
tè (m) *tea*
tè nero (m) *black tea*
tè verde (m) *green tea*
temperatura (f) *temperature*
tempestoso/a *stormy*
tempo *time*
tempo (m) *weather*
tempo libero (m) *leisure*
tenda (f) *tent*
tenda veneziana (f)
Venetian blind
tennis (m) *tennis*
tergicristallo (m)
windshield wiper
terminal (m) *terminal*
termometro (m) *thermometer*
termostato (m) *thermostat*
terremoto (m) *earthquake*
terreno (m) *soil*
tessuto (m) *fabric*
test di gravidanza (m)
pregnancy test
testa (f) *head*
testimone (m/f) *witness*
tetto (m) *roof*
thermos (m) *vacuum flask*
tiepido *warm*
tiglio (m) *lime*
timido/a *shy*
timone (m) *oar*
toga (f) *robe*
tonno (m) *tuna*
torace (m) *chest*

torcia (f) *flashlight*
tornire to turn
torsolo (m) *core*
tosse (f) *cough*
tostapane (m) *toaster*
tovagliolo (m) *napkin*
tra *between*
traffico (m) *traffic*
traghetto (m) *ferry*
tram (m) *tram*
tramezzino (m) *sandwich*
tramonto (m) *sunset*
trancio (m) *steak*
trasporti (m pl) *transportation*
travelers check (m)
traveler's check
tre *three*
treno (m) *train*
trenta *thirty*
treppiede (m) *tripod*
triste *sad*
tritato/a *crushed*
troppo *too*
trota (f) *trout*
trovare to find
trucco (m) *makeup*
T-shirt (f) *t-shirt*
tu *you*
tubetto (m) *tube*
tuffarsi to dive
turista (m/f) *tourist*
tuta subacquea (f) *wetsuit*
tutti *every*
tutto/i *all*
TV satellitare (f)
satellite TV

U

uccelli (m pl) *birds*
ufficio *office*
ufficio del turismo (m)
tourist information office
ufficio di cambio (m)

currency exchange
**ufficio informazioni turistiche
(m)** *tourist information*
ufficio oggetti smarriti (m)
lost property
ufficio postale (m)
post office
ultimo/a *last*
umido/a *humid*
un poco *a little*
undici *eleven*
unghia (f) *nail*
uniforme *uniform*
università (f) *university*
uno/a *one*
uomo (m) *man*
uragano (m) *hurricane*
urgente *urgent*
usare *to use*
uscita (f) *exit*
uscita di emergenza (f)
emergency exit
uscita d'imbarco (f)
boarding gate
utile *useful*

V

vacanza (f) *vacation*
valigetta (f) *briefcase*
valigia (f) *suitcase*
valore (m) *value*
valuta estera (f)
foreign currency
vasca (f) *bathtub*
vaschetta (f) *tub*
vassoio (m) *tray*
vecchio/a *old*
vedere *to see*
vegetariano/a *vegetarian*
vela (f) *sailing*
veloce *fast; quick*
vendere *to sell*
venerdì *Friday*

venire *to come*
venti *twenty*
ventilatore (m) *fan*
ventoso/a *windy*
veramente *really*
verde *green*
verdura (f) *vegetables*
vero *correct*
versare *to pay in*
verso *towards*
vescica (f) *blister*
vespa (f) *wasp*
veterinario/a (m/f) *veterinarian*
vetro (m) *glass*
via (f) *street; way*
viaggio (m) *travel*
viale (m) *avenue*
vicino *close (near)*
vicino a *beside; by; next to*
videogioco (m) *video game*
vidimare *to validate*
vigneto (m) *vineyard*
villaggio (m) *village*
vincere *to win*
vino (m) *wine*
viola *purple*
violenza carnale (f) *rape*
viottolo (m) *path*
virus (m) *virus*
visita (f) *consultation*
visita guidata (f)
guided tour
visitatore (m) *visitor*
viso (m) *face*
vista (f) *view*
visto (m) *visa*
vitamine (f pl)
vitamins
voi *you (pl)*
volante (f) *police car*
volare *to fly*
volere *to want*
volo (m) *flight*

volume (m) *volume*
vomitare *to vomit*
vongola (f) *clam*

W, Y, Z

whisky (m) *whiskey*
wifi (m) *Wi-Fi*
wurstel (m) *sausage*
yacht (m) *yacht*
yoga (m) *yoga*
yogurt (m) *yogurt*
zaino (m) *backpack*
zanzara (f) *mosquito*
zanzariera (f)
 mosquito net
zenzero (m) *ginger*
zero *zero*
zia (f) *aunt*
zio (m) *uncle*
zona (f) *zone*

zoo (m) *zoo*
zucca Butternut (f)
 butternut squash
zucchina (f) *zucchini*

ACKNOWLEDGMENTS

ORIGINAL EDITION

Senior Editors Simon Tuite, Angela Wilkes
Editorial Assistant Megan Jones
US Editor Margaret Parrish
Senior Art Editor Vicky Short
Art Editor Mandy Earey
Production Editor Phil Sergeant
Production Controller Inderjit Bhullar
Managing Editor Julie Oughton
Managing Art Editor Louise Dick
Art Director Bryn Walls
Associate Publisher Liz Wheeler
Publisher Jonathan Metcalf

**Produced for Dorling Kindersley by
SP Creative Design**
Editor Heather Thomas
Designer Rolando Ugolino
**Language content for Dorling
Kindersley by
First Edition Translations Ltd**
Translator Esmerelda Lines
Editor Gabriella Barra
Typesetting Essential Typesetting

Dorling Kindersley would also like to thank the following for their help in the preparation of the original and revised editions of this book: Isabelle Elkaim and Melanie Fitzgerald of First Edition Translations Ltd; Elma Aquino, Mandy Earey, and Meenal Goel for design assistance; Amelia Collins, Nicola Hodgson, Isha Sharma, Janashree Singha, Nishtha Kapil, and Neha Ruth Samuel for editorial assistance; Claire Bowers, Lucy Claxton, and Rose Horridge in the DK Picture Library; Adam Brackenbury, Vânia Cunha, Almudena Diaz, Maria Elia, John Goldsmid, Sonia Pati, Phil Sergeant, and Louise Waller for DTP assistance.

PICTURE CREDITS

The publisher would like to thank the following for their kind permission to reproduce their photographs:
Key: a (above); b (below/bottom); c (centre); l (left); r (right); t (top)
Alamy Images: Alvey & Towers Picture Library p113 cb; PhotoSpin, Inc p38 crb; Tetra Images p20; **Alamy Stock Photo:** Cultura RM p51 br; **Courtesy of Renault:** p26–27 t; **Getty Images:** Reggie Casagrande p148; **PunchStock:** Moodboard p8; **iStockphoto.com:** Mustang_79 p4; **123RF.com:** Cobalt p108 cr; Norman Kin Hang Chan / Bedo p109 clb; Cobalt p134 clb; Cobalt p156 br.

All other images © **Dorling Kindersley**
For further information see: www.dkimages.com

NUMBERS

1 uno *oonoh*	7 sette *settay*	13 tredici *traydeechee*	19 diciannove *deechanovay*	70 settanta *settantah*
2 due *dooeh*	8 otto *ottoh*	14 quattordici *kwattordeechee*	20 venti *ventee*	80 ottanta *ottantah*
3 tre *tray*	9 nove *novay*	15 quindici *kweendeechee*	30 trenta *trentah*	90 novanta *novantah*
4 quattro *kwattroh*	10 dieci *deeaychee*	16 sedici *sedeechee*	40 quaranta *kwarantah*	100 cento *chentoh*
5 cinque *cheenkway*	11 undici *oondeechee*	17 diciasette *deechasettay*	50 cinquanta *cheenkwantah*	1,000 mille *meelay*
6 sei *say*	12 dodici *dodeechee*	18 diciotto *deechottoh*	60 sessanta *sessantah*	

ORDINAL NUMBERS

first primo *preemoh*	**fourth** quarto *kwartoh*	**seventh** settimo *setteemoh*	**tenth** decimo *decheemoh*
second secondo *sekondoh*	**fifth** quinto *kweentoh*	**eighth** ottavo *otahvoh*	**twentieth** ventesimo *ventezeemoh*
third terzo *tertsoh*	**sixth** sesto *sestoh*	**ninth** nono *nonoh*	